MATCH ANNUAL 2004

MATCH Editor > Simon Caney   **Art Director** > Darryl Tooth   **Annual Editor** > Ian Foster   **Assistant Editor** > Kevin Hughes
Production Editor > James Bandy   **Deputy Production Editor** > Kevin Pettman   **Senior Writer** > Giles Milton
Sub-Editor/Writers > Mark Bailey, Darren Cross   **Senior Designer** > Martin Barry   **Designer** > Calum Booth
Photographer > Phil Bagnall   **Cartoonist** > Russ Carvell   **And the rest of the MATCH team** > Dawn Brown & Isobel Cardew

MATCH BRITAIN'S BEST-SELLING FOOTBALL MAGAZINE!
Bushfield House, Orton Centre, Peterborough PE2 5UW ★ Tel: (01733) 237111
Fax: (01733) 288150 ★ e-mail: match.magazine@emap.com

>PLANET FOOTY!<

DID YOU KNOW?

Former Sunderland and Republic Of Ireland striker Niall Quinn has found a new career - as a caddy for golf pro Philip Walton!

FLASH GITS!

Our favourite players are the ones who show off all the time with their amazing tricks and flicks! But who's the flashiest footballer around? MATCH looks at the top contenders...

RONALDINHO

TRICKS!
Against England in the World Cup in 2002, Ronnie put Ashley Cole on his backside with a wicked step-over. Little Ron has certainly got the skills to pay the bills!

FREE-KICKS!
Remember the one against England? Course you do! Apparently, team-mate Cafu told Ron that David Seaman was off his line in that game just before Ron lobbed him!

STYLE!
He looks like a right weirdo, and he admitted himself that he's as ugly as a baboon's backside. But fair play to the lad – he's got a bit of style and swagger about him, even if his front teeth do scrape along the ground!

SHOW-OFFINESS!
The goofball Brazilian demonstrated his well flash ball juggling skills in Nike's quality Freestyle campaign on TV earlier this year. That's not a bad way to get loads of respect as one of the world's tip-top skillsters!

FLASH RATING:

ROBERTO CARLOS

TRICKS!
Being able to kick the ball harder than anybody in the world is a good start. He also shows typical Brazilian skill on the ball. We'll big him up for that, for starters!

FREE-KICKS!
Carlos is called 'El Hombre Bala' – The Bullet Man – for his rocket free-kicks. He begins his run up miles outside the stadium and his kicks often reach 105 miles per hour. They don't always go in, but who cares!

STYLE!
Carlos is the original free spirit, with a shiny attacking style, a shiny personality and a nice shiny head to boot. What more could you ask for? He's shiny!

SHOW-OFFINESS!
On the pitch Carlos is a fancy ball juggler, with flicks, tricks and neat backheels. But does he do it for fun or does it actually beat his opponents? Well, we reckon it's a bit of both really – and we sure ain't complaining!

FLASH RATING:

HIGH FIVE...

SILLIEST HAIRCUTS: These footy stars have all sported some well dodgy hairstyles over the years!

1. RONALDO

2. DAVID BECKHAM

3. DAVID JAMES

4. JUAN PABLO SORIN

5. RONALDINHO

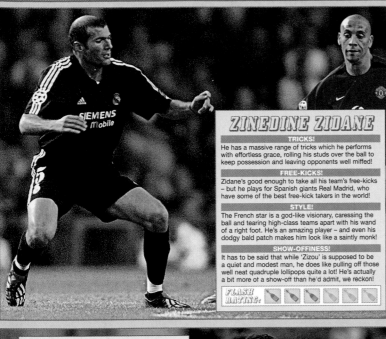

ZINEDINE ZIDANE

TRICKS!
He has a massive range of tricks which he performs with effortless grace, rolling his studs over the ball to keep possession and leaving opponents well miffed!

FREE-KICKS!
Zidane's good enough to take all his team's free-kicks – but he plays for Spanish giants Real Madrid, who have some of the best free-kick takers in the world!

STYLE!
The French star is a god-like visionary, caressing the ball and tearing high-class teams apart with his wand of a right foot. He's an amazing player – and even his dodgy bald patch makes him look like a saintly monk!

SHOW-OFFINESS!
It has to be said that while 'Zizou' is supposed to be a quiet and modest man, he does like pulling off those well neat quadruple lollipops quite a lot! He's actually a bit more of a show-off than he'd admit, we reckon!

FLASH RATING:

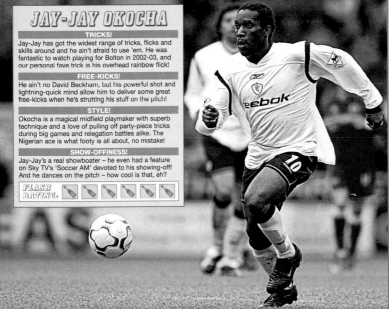

JAY-JAY OKOCHA

TRICKS!
Jay-Jay has got the widest range of tricks, flicks and skills around and he ain't afraid to use 'em. He was fantastic to watch playing for Bolton in 2002-03, and our personal fave trick is his overhead rainbow flick!

FREE-KICKS!
He ain't no David Beckham, but his powerful shot and lightning-quick mind allow him to deliver some great free-kicks when he's strutting his stuff on the pitch!

STYLE!
Okocha is a magical midfield playmaker with superb technique and a love of pulling off party-piece tricks during big games and relegation battles alike. The Nigerian ace is what footy is all about, no mistake!

SHOW-OFFINESS!
Jay-Jay's a real showboater – he even had a feature on Sky TV's 'Soccer AM' devoted to his showing-off! And he dances on the pitch – how cool is that, eh?

FLASH RATING:

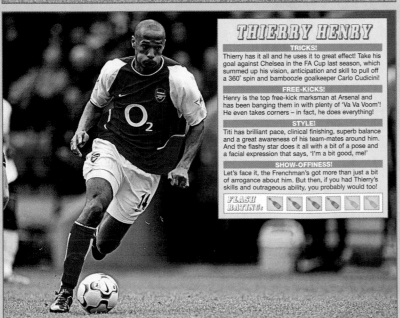

THIERRY HENRY

TRICKS!
Thierry has it all and he uses it to great effect! Take his goal against Chelsea in the FA Cup last season, which summed up his vision, anticipation and skill to pull off a 360° spin and bamboozle goalkeeper Carlo Cudicini!

FREE-KICKS!
Henry is the top free-kick marksman at Arsenal and has been banging them in with plenty of 'Va Va Voom'! He even takes corners – in fact, he does everything!

STYLE!
Titi has brilliant pace, clinical finishing, superb balance and a great awareness of his team-mates around him. And the flashy star does it all with a bit of a pose and a facial expression that says, 'I'm a bit good, me!'

SHOW-OFFINESS!
Let's face it, the Frenchman's got more than just a bit of arrogance about him. But then, if you had Thierry's skills and outrageous ability, you probably would too!

FLASH RATING:

WELCOME TO THE 2004 ANNUAL FROM MATCHMAN!

MATCHMAN SAYS: "Biggedy biggedy big-up to ya for buying da wicked 2004 MATCH Annual! You is gonna get plenty of me being wicked, loadsa toppedy-top footy stars, posters, quizzes an' loads an' loads more that I can't even begin to tell ya 'bout! Dis will be a big year of footy action wiv da Champs League final, FA Cup final, Premiership an' da Euro 2004 Championships in Portugal! Course, I is gonna be there at every massive game, but if ya can't be wiv me, then ya can always pick up a copy of MATCH to keep up with all the latest stuff every week. Anyways, enjoy da Annual and I'll see you lot every Tuesday in MATCH. Peace out!"

RUUD STILL LOVES BECKS!

As far as Ruud van Nistelrooy is concerned, Davie Becks is gone but not forgotten at Manchester United. The striker thrived on the England skipper's crosses, so when Becks went to Real Madrid, Ruud had only sweet memories!

"I can only speak for myself, but I miss him as a man, as a guy in the dressing-room and as a player on the pitch," he said. "It was great to play alongside him!"

Of course, the two are now big rivals in the Champions League and Van Nistelrooy knows what to worry about if United face Real – Beckham's magical right peg!

"Everyone knows about his right foot – there is a kind of magic that comes out of it. It was fantastic to be with him for two years and that is what I'll keep in my mind." Oh stop it, Ruud boy. We're welling up with tears here!

YOUR CLUB'S BADGE EXPLAINED!

MATCH reveals the crazy story behind all those little details on your favourite club's badge!
JUVENTUS

TWO STARS!
Juve have two stars to commemorate the winning of 27 championships. They were awarded one after winning ten and another after reaching 20 titles!

CROWN
This represents the grandness of the club that is the Old Lady Of Turin. Juve see themselves as Italy's biggest and most important club, hence the crown.

BLACK AND WHITE
The black and white colours are due to a mix-up in 1903, when Juve ordered pink shirts from Notts County but got sent black and white shirts instead!

HORSE
The horse represents the badge of Italian car company Fiat and its owners – the Agnelli family. The family symbol is a black bucking horse, and the Agnellis happen to own Juventus Football Club!

DID YOU KNOW?
When Milene Domingues was Ronaldo's girlfriend, she did 55,187 keepie-uppies in nine hours and six minutes!

RU... CRICKET OR FOOTY?

Sadly, a lot of people like to stand around all day in white trousers chasing after a red ball instead of playing footy! But when it comes to the crunch, which one are you?

A		B
The Ashes	V	Ashley Cole
West Indies	V	West Ham
Wickets	V	Michael Ricketts
Brian Lara	V	Dwight Yorke
Wicket Keeper	V	Goalkeeper
A Fielder	V	Anfield
Trent Bridge	V	Wayne Bridge
Leg Before Wicket	V	Legwinski
Stumps	V	Alan Stubbs
Silly point	V	8-8

Mostly A
You're a whites-wearing enemy of footy! Hitting a red ball with a lump of wood isn't sport!
Mostly B
Footy fanatic! You know where it's at and you certainly know to kick it is better than cricket!

DAMIEN DUFF IN WESTLIFE

DEY WERE FLYIN' WIDDOUT WINGERS 'TIL I CAME ALONG!

Pop Idol!
FOOTY STYLE!

If the top footy stars were pop idols, who would they be? MATCH knows!

Loads of famous pop stars – like Robbie Williams, Blue and even Mis-teeq – enjoy a cheeky kickabout in their spare time, so why shouldn't our footy stars have a go at singing and making it big in the music charts?

Let's face it, if fools with the talent of Gareth Gates, Bob The Builder and Ron Atkinson can make a hit song, surely some of our ultra-gifted footy stars would be able to mix it up in the pop world! So if footy players were pop stars, who would they be? Here's MATCH's crazy search for the pop idols of the footy world!

YE SING LIKE POSH. OCH, TERRIBLE!
OCH! THAT'S SHORCKIN', SON!
THE JUDGES

I'M BLONDE, BAD AN' I AIN'T CLEANIN' OUT ME CLOSET, MUM! BITE ME!
ALAN SMITH AS EMINEM

CHECK ME BLING BLING JEWELLERY! BUT I'M STILL RIO FROM DA BLOCK, INNIT?
YO, JT IN DA HOUSE. I'M FEELIN' IT, BABY!
JOHN TERRY AS JUSTIN TIMBERLAKE
RIO FERDINAND AS J-LO

HIGH FIVE...

FOOTY UGLY MUGS: This lot won't be signing modelling contracts soon, and that's a fact!

1. LUKE CHADWICK

2. MARTIN KEOWN

3. GARETH SOUTHGATE

4. BRETT ORMEROD

5. PHIL NEVILLE

OW! SHAMON. OOH-HOO! CHIKKA-OW!

RONALDINHO AS MICHAEL JACKSON

EH MICHAEL, I'M THE KOP IDOL ROUND ERE, LA!

SHUT IT, STEVIE! IT'S POP IDOL NOT KOP IDOL, YA SCALLY!

MICHAEL OWEN & STEVEN GERRARD IN ATOMIC KITTEN

I JUST CAN'T GET FLAMIN' GOALS OUTTA ME 'EAD, SPORT!

HARRY KEWELL AS KYLIE MINOGUE

SOUND. D'YA WANNA FIGHT, EH BRUV?

CITEH RULE! WHAT YA THINK, OUR KID?

GARY AND PHIL NEVILLE IN OASIS

WHAT'S GOING ON IN THE MIND OF...

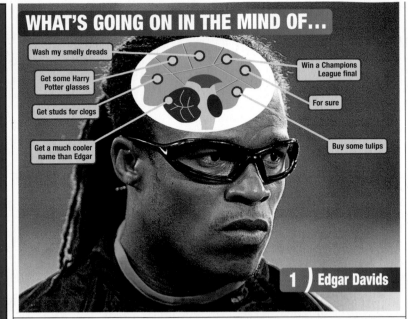

Wash my smelly dreads

Get some Harry Potter glasses

Get studs for clogs

Get a much cooler name than Edgar

Win a Champions League final

For sure

Buy some tulips

1 Edgar Davids

THE ONES THAT GOT AWAY!

Players like Michael Owen, Paul Scholes and Ashley Cole have all made it through trials at big clubs to become top Premiership stars. So the scouts who first spotted them as promising youngsters were proved right! But loads of other stars have been turned away by clubs for not being good enough – only to come back and embarrass the silly coaches who couldn't see their potential! This list of stars (right) either got turned away before they had a chance to show what they could do, or were ignored by clubs after being recommended by scouts. If only the clubs could have seen into the future!

John O'Shea	> Liverpool
Owen Hargreaves	> Everton
David Beckham	> Tottenham
Michael Tonge	> Man. United
Raul	> Atletico Madrid
Carlo Cudicini	> AC Milan
Ryan Giggs	> Man. City
Wayne Rooney	> Liverpool
Andy Cole	> Arsenal
James McEveley	> Everton
Damien Duff	> Liverpool
Santiago Canizares	> Real Madrid

SEE YOU JIMMY!

Chelsea striker Jimmy Floyd Hasselbaink is hiding somewhere in this crowd shot, but can you spot the cheeky Dutchman?

DID YOU KNOW?

As well as English, there were 59 other nationalities
playing in the Premiership last season!

WHAT THE HECK IS FUTBOL?

Now, we know footy has never really taken off in America – probably because their version involves wearing lots of armour and chasing a weird-shaped ball around – but calling our beautiful game 'Futbol' takes the bloomin' biscuit! As if trying to get away with calling it 'soccer' for years wasn't bad enough, 'Futbol' is the new American term for the wicked game we all know and love!

Apparently, footy isn't exciting enough for sophisticated American audiences, so our friends across the pond have come up with different ways to spice the game up – but their suggestions are well weird! First off, they'd like to chop the pitch in half so that the players don't have to run too far in the match, and then add a goal to each side of the pitch, making four goals in total! Confused? You should be, but the wackiness from the Yanks doesn't stop there. Oh no!

Other ideas include doing away with fouls so players can be crunched when they've got the ball, reducing the game to 60 minutes so that the fans don't get too bored, and even awarding seven points for a goal instead of just the one! You can just imagine seeing the ridiculous scoreline coming in on a Saturday afternoon – Arsenal 35–28 Liverpool! Yanks, you've gotta love 'em, ain't ya?

ARSENAL 35
LIVERPOOL 28

WHICH FOOTY

Have you ever pretended to be your favourite player while having a kickabout with your mates? Of course you have! Well, now you can find out which superstar you really are by taking MATCH's simple test! Are you flash like Becks, angry like Keano, sensible like Owen, a big kid like Rooney – or an ancient pro like Seaman? Try our test and all will be revealed!

10 WAYS ARSENAL CAN WIN THE TITLE BACK!

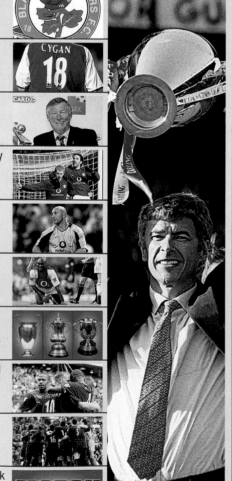

1 Avoid Blackburn, who did the double over The Gunners in 2002-03!

2 Keep defender Pascal Cygan out of the side as much as possible!

3 Don't get involved with Fergie's mind games!

4 Buy Ruud van Nistelrooy and Paul Scholes from Manchester United!

5 Convince Sir Alex to keep playing dodgy 'keeper Fabien Barthez!

6 Hope that big defender Sol Campbell doesn't get suspended again!

7 Forget the Champions League, the FA Cup and the Carling Cup!

8 Clone Thierry Henry and Patrick Vieira!

9 Get another winning streak going!

10 Read MATCH every week to get the lowdown on all the opposition!

MATCH

AIN'T YOU TWO BROTHERS?

DIE HARD, PUNK!

JAAP STAM   BRUCE WILLIS

HIGH FIVE...

CRAZIEST 'KEEPERS: These dudes between the sticks are all as mad as a box of frogs!

1. FABIEN BARTHEZ   2. RUSTU RECBER   3. OLIVER KAHN   4. PETER ENCKELMAN   5. JOSE CHILAVERT

WHICH FOOTY PLAYER ARE YOU?

1 You're looking to buy a new house – what sort of thing will you go for?

a) A castle made of gold and diamonds, surrounded by a moat to keep the Press out!

b) Somewhere near a nice big field so your dog can have great walkies every day!

c) A whole street of sensibly priced houses for your entire family. Nothing too flashy, though!

d) Move out? You'd miss your mum's cooking too much! There's no way you're doing that!

e) That old fogies' home at the bottom of the road looks really nice and quiet!

2 You're house is great, but it's miles from training – how do you get there?

a) Take the private helicopter and land it right in the gaffer's parking spot!

b) Go in the massive monster truck, just in case anyone gets in your way!

c) The Jaguar, obviously. A flash sports car or a motorbike would be too much like fun!

d) It'll have to be the BMX, but there's no way your team-mates are getting a backie!

e) Nothing too fast – driving over 30mph makes you feel very uncomfortable!

3 You fancy having a new hairdo, but what style will you pick?

a) A mohawk... no, a mullet... braids! It really doesn't matter – everyone will just copy you!

b) You don't want any stray hair getting in the way, so it has to be a skinhead! Grrrrrr!

c) Nothing too risky – a short back and sides will sort you out nicely!

d) You're still praying for the day you can grow some manly sideboards!

e) Must remember to get some new hair dye to hide the grey spots on your ponytail!

4 The Press want to know if you'll be moving clubs – what do you do?

a) Go on holiday to America and look moody whenever you spot a bloke with a camera!

b) Get red in the face with rage and chase the Press down the street!

c) Issue a statement saying you love the club you're at and there's no way you'll leave!

d) Don't say anything. Your manager doesn't let you speak to anyone – ever!

e) Tell them that you fancy playing here for at least another season, even though you're 106!

5 You need some new clothes – what will you buy at the shops?

a) A flashy Armani suit. But make sure that it matches your favourite sarong!

b) Just shorts and a T-shirt – the bad weather doesn't scare you one bit!

c) Another England tracksuit!

d) Your mum usually gets your clothes. Oh well, how about a Spider-Man outfit? Yeah!

e) Some comfortable slippers, a shirt, tie and smoking jacket. You'll be the envy of all the old duffers in the home dressed in that!

6 After a bad game, the gaffer kicks a boot at you. What do you do?

a) Storm out. Then get the biggest plaster money can buy and stick it over the scratch!

b) Clothesline the manager and tell the Press that you'll never play for the club again!

c) Nothing. You're sure it was an accident!

d) Cry for a bit, then tell the gaffer you'll only be his friend again if he lets you have his brand new Bay Blade to play with!

e) Seek medical advice. A blow like that could really hurt a man of your age!

WHICH FOOTY PLAYER ARE YOU?

MOSTLY Es

David Seaman

Despite making your debut in 1902, you're sure you've still got what it takes to play at the top. Nobody told you that ponytails went out of fashion, but you don't really care – the hairdo's a wig anyway!

MOSTLY Ds

Wayne Rooney

You might only be a kid, but you're still one of the best players around. A career full of England caps and plenty of goals awaits you – if only you could pass your driving test so you can get rid of that cruddy BMX!

MOSTLY Cs

Michael Owen

You're Mr Sensible and you know it! You've been a great player for your club and country, the fans love you, the manager loves you and your team-mates love you! But please, lighten up just a little bit!

MOSTLY Bs

Roy Keane

Grrrrrrr! You don't take any stick from anyone and you're not afraid to tell the world what you think about anything and everything. You've mellowed out a bit lately, but that old spark is still there!

MOSTLY As

David Beckham

You're the most famous player in the world and a fashion icon! You're married to a pop star and have more wonga than the Queen! You just wish the newspapers would leave you alone for once in your life!

TRANSFERS THAT SHOULD HAPPEN...

> HARRY SAYS I COULD STILL DO A JOB UP FRONT!

No.23: Gary Lineker to Portsmouth.

CARLOS' COMEDY CORNER!

Real Madrid's mighty midget full-back Roberto Carlos is a man of many talents. He's faster than a Ferrari, more powerful than a steam train, and he's got more tricks than the inside of a wizard's sleeve! But did you know that the bonkers Brazilian legend is a comedy genius, too?

Nope, neither did we until we met up with him in Madrid to ask him what he thought of David Beckham becoming his new team-mate. **"Finally, Real Madrid now have two handsome players,"** he said. As MATCH wondered what he was on about, a chuckling Carlos added: **"Previously, the only good looking guy in the squad was me!"**

Considering that Robby C is more of a Luke Chadwick than a Luis Figo, we soon worked out he was just having a laugh with us! Well he was, wasn't he?

DODD SCORES 140!

Southampton defender Jason Dodd doesn't usually hit the headlines for his scoring ability for The Saints, so how the heck did the veteran full-back manage to hit 140 in a single match? Surely we can't be talking about footy, can we?

Nah, of course not! While most players spent the summer trying to improve their golf handicap on the course, Saints star Dodd showed he's an all-round sportsman by playing cricket! The full-back helped his club, Flamingos, to an easy victory by walloping ball after ball over the boundary, managing to clock up almost half of his team's 333 runs! Not happy with that though, Doddsy then had a dabble at bowling and took five wickets! Maybe you're in the wrong sport, Doddsy!

---

jobs for the boys

If footy stars weren't in the game, what would they do for a living instead? MATCH takes a wild guess!

> NOW THAT IS WHAT I CALL VA VA VOOM, NON?

THIERRY HENRY AS... AN OLYMPIC SPRINTER

When I were a boy...

> FORGET FERRARIS! WHEN I WAS A LAD, PLAYERS GOT AROUND ON PENNY FARTHINGS!

DID YOU KNOW?

Aston Villa's Olof Mellberg was the only player to play in every minute of every Premiership game last season!

IS THE PREM THE BEST IN THE WORLD?

5 Reasons why the Premiership kicks butt!

1 The action is always fast and furious in the Premiership – so no messing about with eight defenders like in Italy. Sometimes there's no defending going on at all – just ask Manchester City fans!

2 The Premiership is full of top young players like Wayne Rooney, Jermaine Jenas and John O'Shea, and they'll still be playing at the top level in ten years' time!

3 There's not so much diving in the Prem as in some of Europe's leagues. Players in England just don't do it – well, except for Ruud van Nistelrooy that is!

4 Some of the craziest gaffers in the world work in the Premiership, like football boot-lobbing Sir Alex Ferguson and Arsene Wenger, who can't see anything!

5 We've got all the daft footy pundits! Big Ron Atkinson is a legend on ITV – after all, where would we be without his silly phrases!

5 Reasons why the Premiership is pure pants!

1 Some of the very best players in the world play in Italy and Spain! There's Ronaldo, Figo, Raul, Roberto Carlos, Beckham, Zidane, Shevchenko and Vieri. Phew!

2 Because of the well nice weather, you can go and watch a game in Spain or Italy wearing just a T-shirt. Try doing that in Manchester in January or February!

3 The Premiership might have some pretty good stadiums, but they don't come close to the world-famous Santiago Bernabeu, where Real Madrid play, or the San Siro – home to the Milan clubs!

4 La Liga is well hard to win, and although Real are usually at the top, it's often a close race between four or five teams. It's not like that in the Premiership these days!

5 The Prem has derbies in Manchester, London, Liverpool and Birmingham, but they're nowt compared to Real Madrid v Barça, or AC v Inter!

CONCLUSION!

FORGET THE REST, THE PREM IS STILL THE BEST!

THE FOOTY RICH

Everyone knows that top footballers – as well as some pretty rubbish ones – earn loads of dosh nowadays! But do you know just how much wonga Ronaldo and the rest are taking home in their pay packets every week?

Well, lucky for you lot, MATCH has spent ages number-crunching on our calculator to find the five richest footballers! And because we know you're all dead nosy, we've even worked out roughly how much cash Becks and the boys earn from their clubs each week! Bling-o-rama!

1) DAVID BECKHAM

Bling-bling rating:	£££££
Weekly wage:	£94,000
Sponsorship deals:	£106,000
Wonga total:	**£200,000 per week**

England captain and Real Madrid star Becks earns more moolah from sponsorship deals than he does from actually playing footy, with huge companies like Pepsi and Adidas flashing the cash to put his face to their worldwide products. Becks has well over £10 million a year pouring into his bulging bank account, which should help to pay for some of his flashy motors, huge houses, well-blingin' jewellery and ultra-expensive threads!

2) ZINEDINE ZIDANE

Bling-bling rating:	££££
Weekly wage:	£120,000
Sponsorship deals:	£60,000
Wonga total:	**£180,000 per week**

'Zizou' became the world's most expensive signing ever when he left Juventus to join Real Madrid for £48 million in 2001, and immediately picked up a massive pay rise, as his weekly wage shot up to well over the £100,000 mark! The France international is not as high-profile as his team-mate David Beckham, but both of them share the same boot sponsor, Adidas. All his deals and massive wages give Zidane the number two spot in our rich list!

Peace and Riise!

Liverpool's war-hating John Arne Riise campaigns for peace in the world!

> I'M WATERSKIING FOR WORLD PEACE, FOOTY DUDES!

BRITISH SAMBA BOYS!

If you've grown up watching the wickedly skills of Rivaldo, Roberto Carlos and Ronaldinho, you've probably dreamed about following in their footsteps. Well, for two young English lads, that dream has become a reality! After training with the Brazilian Soccer School Futebol de Salao in their home town of Leeds for four years, brothers Irfan and Mohammed Akram have signed pro contracts with top club Resende in Brazil!

The lads were offered a trial during a trip to Rio last summer, and returned to sign permanent deals after doing their A-Levels in August 2003! **"We played in a match at Resende and they said we could come back!"** said a very happy Mohammed. So who knows, the next Ronaldo might be English. Flash, eh?

> ANY CHANCE OF GETTING RIO TO RIO, THEN?

HIGH FIVE...

FOOTBALL MIDGETS: There are loads of pocket rockets in footy, but these are some of the best!

1. ROBERTO CARLOS

2. ASHLEY COLE

3. JUNINHO

4. GIANFRANCO ZOLA

5. PABLO AIMAR

LIST!

3) RONALDO

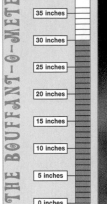

Bling-bling rating:	£££££
Weekly wage:	£100,000
Sponsorship deals:	£50,000
Wonga total:	£150,000 per week

Brazil ace Ronaldo may be a bit on the flabby side, but he's not half as fat as his wallet – which is massive! After an amazing World Cup – where he won the Golden Boot – the striker bagged himself a move to Real Madrid, who doubled his wages! Add to that a sponsorship deal with Nike and you've got one very rich footy player – although he obviously spends a lot of his spare cash on food!

4) RIO FERDINAND

Bling-bling rating:	£££££
Weekly wage:	£80,000
Sponsorship deals:	£40,000
Wonga total:	£120,000 per week

Manchester United made Ferdinand the most expensive defender in history when they shelled out the best part of £30 million to convince Leeds United to part with the England centre-back. A huge basic wage at Old Trafford, and massive deals with Nike and Ben Sherman to name just two, earn Rio in excess of £6 million every year. He's still only young and his earnings potential is only going to rise!

5) ALESSANDRO DEL PIERO

Bling-bling rating:	£££££
Weekly wage:	£70,000
Sponsorship deals:	£50,000
Wonga total:	£120,00 per week

Del Piero is the jewel in the Juventus crown – as his wages prove! Forget Rivaldo, Henry, Totti, Figo, Owen and Raul – those guys all earn less cash than the Serie A star who has been working his magic in Turin for the last ten years. Alex led Juventus to another league title last season, as well as the 2003 Champions League final against AC Milan. His weekly wage is almost as much as MATCHMAN's, and that's well massive!

DON'T BE SO RUUD!

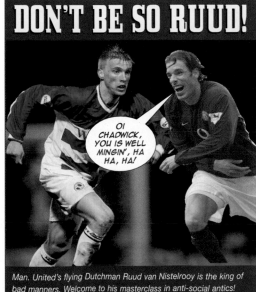

> OI CHADWICK, YOU IS WELL MINGIN', HA HA, HA!

Man. United's flying Dutchman Ruud van Nistelrooy is the king of bad manners. Welcome to his masterclass in anti-social antics!
THIS TIME: STARING AT UGLY PEOPLE!

THE BOUFFANT-O-METER

- 35 inches
- 30 inches
- 25 inches
- 20 inches
- 15 inches
- 10 inches
- 5 inches
- 0 inches

> HOLY PIZZERIA! IF MY HAIRDO KEEPS A-GROWING LIKE THEEES, I WILL BE TALLER THAN THE TOWER OF PISA!

GIANLUIGI BOUFFANT!

It's hair crazy with the Juventus goalkeeper and his amazing growing barnet!

IS GERRARD DIOUF'S DAD?

Now we all know that gaffers like to stick up for their players – especially if they've shelled out loads of dosh to sign them – but Gerrard Houllier really got us thinking after talking about striker El-Hadji Diouf!

The Liverpool boss was sticking up for the Senegal superstar after a spitting incident in last season's UEFA Cup clash with Celtic. **"I forgive him. It's like when you have a child who makes a mistake, even if it's a big mistake,"** explained the Anfield gaffer. **"You try to understand and try to explain to him – that's because he is your child!"**

Well, that explains why Diouf kept playing for the first team in 2002-03 despite being pants – he's Gerard's long lost son! Well, probably not, but we reckon it's as good a reason as any!

BERGER'S 🍔 BURGERS!

It's munch-out time with Portsmouth's fast-food obsessed Czech star!

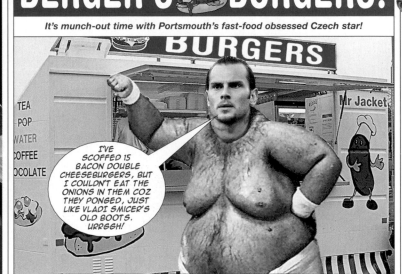

TEA
POP
WATER
COFFEE
CHOCOLATE

BURGERS

Mr Jacket

> I'VE SCOFFED 15 BACON DOUBLE CHEESEBURGERS, BUT I COULDN'T EAT THE ONIONS IN THEM COZ THEY PONGED, JUST LIKE VLADI SMICER'S OLD BOOTS. URRGGH!

"You can... quote me on that"

"Marcel will come in for a game and he won't even know who we are playing. He will say to me, 'Baba, who are we playing today?' Then he comes into training during the week and doesn't know what day of the week it is!"
Nippy Chelsea full-back Celestine Babayaro gives us an insight into the weird and wonderful world of Marcel Desailly. Good to see the Chelsea star is always on top of his game, then!

"I can play football now at my level for £500 a month, because I love it so much."
Mad Marcel confirms that he's a bit of a loon, and does his chances of a pay rise at mega-rich Chelsea no good at all! The wife won't be happy with that one, mate!

"I gave away the foul that Leeds scored one goal from – then put the ball into my own net from their free-kick. I don't want to say I lost us the championship, but..."
Arsenal full-back Ashley Cole admits he may have cost The Gunners the Premiership title last season, even though he didn't want to! What is it with footballers saying daft things all the time? They should keep their gobs shut tight!

"It's not nice going into the supermarket when the woman at the checkout is thinking 'dodgy 'keeper'."
England stopper David James tells how he's still struggling to lose his 'Calamity James' tag! Go shopping in disguise then, Jamo!

"All I've ever wanted to do is play football, but I still have to go to college once a week because my dad says so."
Leeds United's wonder kid James Milner knows the boss in his house!

THE UNOFFICIAL & NOT WHOL

Born in London in 1981, Joe Cole came from the back streets of the East End to play for West Ham at

1 Little baby Joe Cole was born on an East End market stall in 1981!

WAAH! I WANNA BE IN WEST 'AM, NOT DA EAST END! WAAH!

2 His mum Pauline looked after him really well...

EAT UP ALL YER COCKLES, LUV, OR THEY'LL BE NO JELLIED EELS FER DESSERT!

3

THIS IS NAFF! I WANNA PLAY FOOTY!

...but he soon got fed up working in the sweaty launderette!

7

WAHAY! I'M DA TRICKIEST TRICKSTER IN TOWN!

He finally got his chance outfield and really showed his class...

8

TRY AN' DO THIS IF YA CAN, EH?

...in fact, he was the most skilful player around!

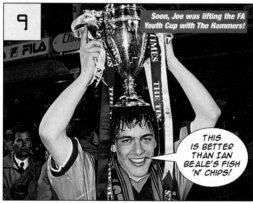

9 Soon, Joe was lifting the FA Youth Cup with The Hammers!

THIS IS BETTER THAN IAN BEALE'S FISH 'N' CHIPS!

13

EVEN PADDINGTON BEAR'S BIGGER THAN ME!

There was only one problem – Joe was only two feet tall!

14

AW C'MON! THAT 'URTS!

Even girls were stronger than him!

15

I'LL TAKE YA ALL ON NOW, EH!

Joe tried everything to get bigger...

19

I REALLY LIKE YOUR SUIT, JOE!

YEAH, I LIKE YOURS TOO, MATE!

Joe was finally bling bling, and started cruising around in style!

20

THIS IS LIKE RUNNIN' ME OWN MARKET STALL!

Soon, Joe became West Ham captain...

21

I WANT MY MUMMY! WAAH!

...but his world was torn apart when The Hammers were relegated in 2003!

HIGH FIVE...

TOP ENGLAND STRIKERS: MATCH looks back at England's best strikers through the generations!

 **1. GEOFF HURST**
 2. GARY LINEKER
 **3. ALAN SHEARER**
 **4. MICHAEL OWEN**
 5. WAYNE ROONEY

LY TRUE STORY OF JOE COLE!

the age of 17, before captaining The Hammers aged just 21! Here's the story of Joey's rise to stardom!

4

WICKED OR WOT? I'M GONNA BE AN 'APPY 'AMMER!

Joe left home to become a trainee at West Ham...

5

...but unfortunately they shoved him in goal!

AW, C'MON YOU GUYS! I'M NOT A 'KEEPER!

6

I'M GONNA BE A TOP FOOTY STAR ONE DAY, I TELL YA!

But Joey was determined to succeed and practised all day!

10

I'VE GOT MORE TRICKS THAN A MAGICIAN'S SLEEVE, INNIT?

Joe burst into the West Ham first team and looked wicked...

11

...even though he was only nine years old! The world was at his feet...

BYE-BYE WALFORD! I'M TAKIN' ON DA WORLD!

12

WOOHOO! I'M AN INGER-LAND ACE!

...and soon Joe was playing a leading role in the England Under-21 side as well!

16

...and even dyed his hair to look hard like Eminem!

BITE ME! I'M A BADASS, DUDE!

17

SO JOEY, SO JOEY GO!

But soon Joe was back to his confident self...

18

'AVE IT!

...and was back to his best for West Ham!

22

SCREAMER!

Joey focused on his England career, and scored his first goal against Serbia-Montenegro...

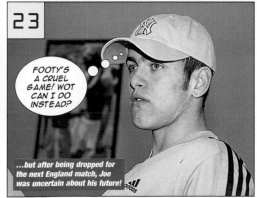

23

FOOTY'S A CRUEL GAME! WOT CAN I DO INSTEAD?

...but after being dropped for the next England match, Joe was uncertain about his future!

24

LUVVERLY JUBBERLY! THIS IS PUKKA! BONJOUR, BONJOUR!

Fortunately, Del Boy came to the rescue and helped him to a future of fame and fortune!

WORLD SUPE

RONALDO
PAGE 16

WAYNE
ROONEY
PAGE 22

RAUL
PAGE 28

R STRIKERS!

ANDRIY SHEVCHENKO PAGE 46

CHRISTIAN VIERI PAGE 68

***MATCH** finds out how the world's best strikers made it to the top!*

Every professional footy player has a different story to tell about how they made it to the top. So MATCH decided to take an exciting look at five of the most deadly strikers in world footy to find out more about their brilliant careers!

Before winning the World Cup and the Spanish title, Ronaldo had many highs and lows – including career-threatening injuries and huge transfers! Everton and England hero Wayne Rooney only ever wanted to play for The Toffees and lead the line for his country – but how did his dreams come true when he was just 17 years old?

Real Madrid ace Raul was a boy wonder too, but his career could have been a lot different if he'd stayed with his first club Atletico Madrid! Dynamic AC Milan star Andriy Shevchenko enjoyed a rapid rise from Dynamo Kiev to Champions League glory, and much-travelled Inter Milan goal machine Christian Vieri went from being a cricket lover to one of the most feared strikers in the world! Check out each of their gripping stories – right here, right now!

WORLD SUPER STRIKERS!

"Congratulations for buying Ronaldo? Thanks, but my grandma would have discovered a talent like that!"

Frank Arnesen, the man who brought Ronaldo to PSV Eindhoven.

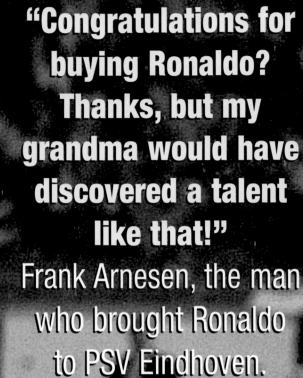

RONALDO

Ronaldo Timeline...

July
TEEN STAR
Joins Brazilian Division Two side Sao Cristovao and nets 36 goals in 54 games.

1991

June
CRUZ-ING
Signs for Cruzeiro, at a cost of just £50,000, and goes on to score 54 goals in 54 games!

1993

March
BRAZIL DEBUT
Makes international debut for Brazil in a 2-1 win over rivals Argentina.

June
WORLD CUP
Flies to the USA with 1994 World Cup squad, but doesn't play as Brazil lift the trophy.

August
PSV BOY
Signs for Dutch side PSV for £4.5 million.

1994

May
TOP SCORER
Finishes his first season in Holland as top scorer, with 35 goals in 37 games.

November
INJURY WOE
Suffers knee injury, having scored 12 goals in 13 games.

1995

May
CUP COMEBACK
Returns to PSV team as a sub in the Dutch Cup final.

July
BARÇA BOY
Joins Bobby Robson's Barcelona for £13.5 million, breaking the world transfer record.

1996

November
TOP AWARD
Named 1996 FIFA World Player Of The Year.

May
EURO JOY
Scores winner in Cup-Winners' Cup final and finishes the season with 33 goals in 38 games.

June
INTER ACE
Signs for Inter Milan for a world record £18 million fee.

December
MORE AWARDS
Wins European Footballer Of The Year award.

1997

FIFA WORLD PLAYER 2002
17 December 200
Palacio de Congresos,

MATCH charts the rise of REAL MADRID superstar RONALDO!

He is The Phenomenon. A boy wonder who became the world's top goalscorer – winning the World Cup, picking up personal awards, suffering major injuries and being involved in one of football's biggest controversies of all time. He is Ronaldo!

The Brazilian star's sensational hat-trick against Man. United was one of the most memorable moments of last season. And the standing ovation he got from the United fans was the ultimate compliment – as he outshone their own hero Ruud van Nistelrooy.

It also marked the 27-year-old's complete recovery from major knee injuries – after finishing as top scorer at the 2002 World Cup and netting twice in the final as he inspired Brazil to the trophy.

If the World Cup marked Big Ron's comeback, that hat-trick against Man. United confirmed he was back to his unstoppable best! Ronaldo has an amazing story that began in the early 1990s, when the young star burst on to the scene in Brazilian football. MATCH takes a look at the career of a football legend who's had the highest highs and the lowest lows!

CAREER FACTFILE

Born: September 22, 1976 in Rio de Janeiro

Nationality: Brazilian

Position: Striker

Height: 6ft

Weight: 12st 0lb

Former clubs: Ramos, Sao Cristovao, Cruzeiro, PSV, Barcelona, Inter Milan

Signed: £24.5 million on August 31, 2002

Real Madrid debut: v Alaves on October 6, 2002

Total Real Madrid games/goals: 45/30 (October 2002 to July 2003)

International caps/goals: Brazil 78/54 (March 1994 to July 2003)

May

CUP WINNER
Scores as Inter win UEFA Cup and finishes with 34 goals in total.

January

FIFA PRIZE
FIFA World Player Of The Year for the second year running.

June

MYSTERY
Despite playing well, suffers mysterious fit before Brazil lose the World Cup final.

1998

September

MAJOR BLOW
Suffers knee troubles which keep him out for most of the Serie A campaign.

October

RED-CARDED
Scores in Milan derby for Inter again AC, but is then sent off.

1999

November

KNEE OP
Suffers another knee injury, against Lecce, which forces him to have surgery in Paris.

April

INJURY HEARTBREAK
Makes his comeback in the Italian Cup final, but goes off after just six minutes with more knee problems.

2000

March

COMEBACK KING
After nearly two years of troubles, Ronaldo returns to action and finishes the Serie A season with an impressive seven goals in ten games.

June

WORLD JOY
Finishes World Cup with eight goals as Brazil win the trophy. Big Ron scores twice in the final.

2002

August

THE REAL DEAL
Joins the superstars at Real Madrid in a £24.5 million deal.

2003

April, 2003

HAT-TRICK HERO
Scores hat-trick as Real knock Man. United out of Europe. Two months later, Real win La Liga and Ron finishes with 23 goals.

1994

JULY BRAZIL WONDER KID!

Ronaldo grew up playing footy on the streets in a poor suburb of Rio de Janeiro. He learnt his skills by playing Futebol de Salão, a small-sided game with a heavy, miniature ball. The young star played for Salão side Ramos and full side Sao Cristovao between 1991 and 1993, but was rejected after a trial at Flamengo. His hard work finally paid off though, as he got a move to top side Cruzeiro in June 1993. Things went brilliantly at his first major club, with Ron scoring 41 goals in 45 matches. This brought him his Brazil debut at just 17 years old against big rivals Argentina. The youngster was then called into the Brazil squad for the 1994 World Cup, held in the USA. He didn't play, but his country won the trophy!

1994

AUGUST GOING DUTCH!

Ronaldo joined PSV Eindhoven in August 1994 and made a huge impact. Despite struggling with the change in weather and food, he had no problems on the pitch and was crowned the top scorer in Holland with 35 goals from 38 games. But after growing three inches and gaining five kilos in just one year at PSV, he suffered the first signs of the serious knee injuries that would blight his later career. He missed four months of the 1995-96 season, having started the new campaign like he finished the last with 12 goals in 13 games. Fortunately, he was able to return in time to pick up a bronze medal with Brazil at the 1996 Olympics. By this point it became clear that PSV couldn't keep him, and after a bidding war, Barcelona snapped him up for a world record £13 million fee.

1996

BARÇA BOY!

Back in the days when Barcelona were the biggest club in Spain, they had the power to attract the top players with ease. Having had the previous Brazilian superstar striker Romario at the Nou Camp, it was almost inevitable that Ronaldo would also become a legend at the Catalan giants. Bobby Robson – then the manager of Barça – had decided to buy Ronaldo instead of Blackburn's Alan Shearer, who would later break the world transfer record by joining Newcastle for £15 million. The decision to go with Ron was a wise one though, as he netted 47 goals in 49 appearances and won the FIFA World Player Of The Year award at the end of 1996. The club ended up lifting the Spanish Cup and the European Cup-Winners' Cup in 1997, with Ronaldo netting the winner! He'd proved himself in the world's second best league of the time, and it wasn't long before one of the big boys from the world's best league came knocking!

1997

INTER THE UNKNOWN!

If Barcelona was a challenge, it was nothing compared to playing in the defence-minded Italian Serie A. That challenge came in 1997, when Inter Milan bid a world record £18 million for Ronaldo. Inter were long-time fans of the Brazilian and it wasn't hard to persuade him to join. Any doubters who questioned how he would handle the physical Italian game soon had their questions answered. The striker, nicknamed 'Il Phenomenon' by Inter fans, quickly showed his class and finished his first season with 32 goals, which made him Serie A's top scorer. The season was a virtual repeat of Ronaldo's first season at Barcelona, as he was named FIFA World Player Of The Year for a second year in a row, as well as picking up the 1997 European Player Of The Year award. What's more, he tasted Euro glory again as Inter won the UEFA Cup with a 3-0 victory over Lazio – with Ron on the scoresheet. He was the biggest player in the world's best league!

1998

JULY MYSTERY!

Ronaldo was billed as the star of the 1998 World Cup and it looked like he would live up to that as he helped Brazil to the final. But on the day of the game, there were rumours he'd suffered a fit the night before and wasn't able to play, but the Brazilians remained tight-lipped. What was going on? The mystery deepened as first he was named on the team sheet, then he was left out, and then he was back in. Finally, the player emerged on to the pitch, looking nervous and subdued. Ronaldo never got going in the game and was a shadow of his former self. France won 3-0 and Ronaldo's mysterious appearance became the subject of massive media speculation. No answers were given, amid wild rumours of the player reacting badly to painkillers or his sponsors stepping in to demand the player took to the field. Whatever really happened, we'll probably never know.

1998

NOVEMBER A WORLD OF PAIN!

Ronaldo's career was brought to a standstill in November 1998 after a reoccurrence of the knee injuries which had blighted his football career. After five months, the doctors at Inter gave him the all-clear to return. And when Ronaldo trotted on to the pitch in the Italian Cup final, he was given a standing ovation by both Inter and Lazio fans – because they all knew what it meant to the Brazilian to be back playing again. Ron looked lean and sharp, and six minutes after coming off the bench he set off on a run at goal. But suddenly, his feet gave way and he crashed to the floor. The striker cried out in pain, clutching that same damaged knee which had given him so many problems. The star was carried off in agony, and in Ronaldo's tears you could see the frustration of a player whose dreams had been totally ripped apart. Was it the end of Ronaldo?

2002

REHABILITATION!

It's said that Ronaldo's injuries come from his time at PSV. While at the Dutch club, he turned from a slight teenager into a bustling, brutal juggernaut of a striker. The club worked hard on his physical strength, and Ron spent hours in the gym, with muscle-building protein supplements to help him to grow. But this may have had bad effects on his teenage body. Growing too fast, too young, Ronaldo's tendons struggled to deal with his new, muscular shape. This is one of the main theories as to why he's suffered so many problems in his knees over the years. Finally, Ronaldo returned in style for Inter in time to finish the season with a flurry of goals, and prove himself fit for the 2002 World Cup finals!

2002

JUNE GUESS WHO'S BACK!

Unlike 1998, Brazil weren't the favourites for the World Cup and Ronaldo wasn't billed as the biggest potential star. But as the games began, it was soon clear that Ron was back in the groove. He scored against Turkey, China and Belgium, twice against Costa Rica and against Turkey in the semis. The final was billed as Ronaldo versus Oliver Khan, the great German 'keeper. But there was only going to be one winner – as Ronaldo scored the first before slotting home a second to secure the World Cup. His tally of eight goals made him the Golden Boot winner as well. The Phenomenon was back in the biggest way possible!

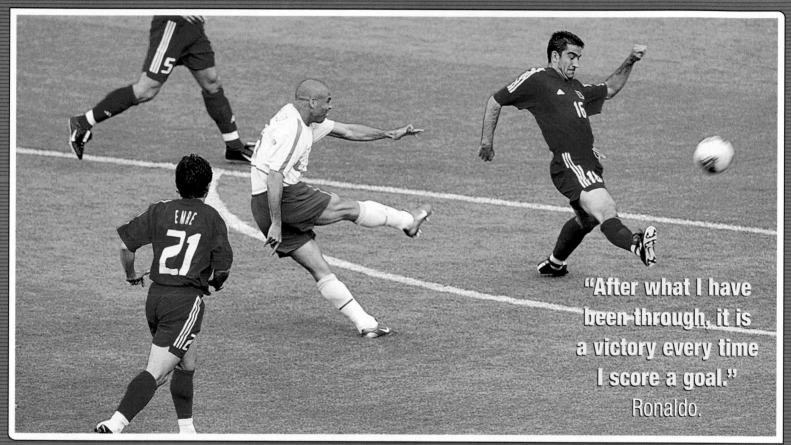

> "After what I have been through, it is a victory every time I score a goal."
> Ronaldo.

JULY REAL GONE KID!

It was soon after the 2002 World Cup that speculation over the future of Ronaldo began. He had re-established himself as football's biggest star, but rumours were flying around that he didn't have a very good relationship with Inter coach Hector Cuper. The first club alerted were Real Madrid, who decided the Inter striker would be their perfect summer signing. The negotiations took ages, but a deal was struck worth around £24.5 million. Inter fans were furious, saying they felt totally betrayed after sticking by the Brazilian during his injuries. Ronaldo, however, was determined to move to Spain and despite the 'Judas' taunts, he joined Real Madrid.

2003

COMING GOOD!

Real fans are fickle – but having the world's best players at their disposal allows them to be picky! So when Ronaldo didn't manage to make the start of the season due to a lack of fitness, the first question marks were raised over his commitment to Real. He scored twice against Alaves on his debut, but the fans were alarmed by his bulky appearance. And Ron didn't seem very popular in the dressing room either – after taking the place of Fernando Morientes, a close friend of Raul. Public criticism by Raul and coach Vicente del Bosque may have stung Ronaldo, but he didn't show it. Ron's performances improved and in the Champions League quarter-final second leg at Old Trafford it all came together. A stunning hat-trick ensured Real's passage to the semis and the big man was back! Most important of all, it won him the love of the fans and his team-mates. Madrid went out in the semi-finals, but Ronaldo secured the Spanish title with two goals in the final game of the season. It was his first league title, but surely not his last!

> PLANET FOOTY! <

DID YOU KNOW?
Sunderland lost a record 15 Premiership games in a row last season!

HEAD-TO-HEAD
RUUD VAN NISTELROOY v THIERRY HENRY

Forget Mike Tyson v Lennox Lewis or Roy Keane v Mick McCarthy, this is the one head-to-head you've all been waiting for – Ruud van Nistelrooy v Thierry Henry! Footy fans spend hours arguing about who's the best striker in England, so MATCH decided to settle the score once and for all!

PACE!

7 9

He might not look that quick, but when Ruud gets going he can really motor! If you don't believe us, just think back to the Arsenal v Man. United clash at Highbury last season, when he left Martin Keown and Sol Campbell in his wake as he raced to score the first!

Thierry Henry is often described as having the pace of an Olympic sprinter – but that doesn't do him justice! There's simply no faster player in the world than the Arsenal striker, who is so quick he makes it look like the opposition are running in slow-mo!

POWER!

9 8

The Premiership is far more physical than La Liga or Serie A, but that doesn't bother Van Nistelrooy! Often used as a lone striker, he specialises in holding off defenders before turning and shooting. He sometimes falls over in the box – but not through lack of strength!

Thierry isn't renowned for his strength, but don't be fooled into thinking he's a wimp! Formerly a winger with both Monaco and Juventus, Henry knows how to take the big challenges. But like Ruud, he also gets his fair share of stick for tumbling too easily.

SKILL!

8 9

Okay, he's not Jay-Jay Okocha, but Ruud's got a few tricks up his sleeve – as Fulham found out when he dribbled past half their team last season! Even when he's running at pace, Ruud's ball control is top class and he can wrong-foot even the best defenders!

Henry can rightly count himself as one of the most skilful players in the Premiership, if not the world. He will often drift out into a wide position during matches, before losing his marker with dazzling footwork and heading for goal. This boy's a real box of tricks!

HEADING!

9 7

Although he bags most goals with his feet, Van The Man weighs in with a few headed goals too! He's not the tallest striker in the world, but he's just as comfortable in the air as he is on the ground, and has proven that a well-timed leap is all it takes to score!

If Thierry has a flaw, it's definitely in the air! Henry's heading ability isn't exactly up to that of other world-class strikers, and it took him over 100 goals before he scored with his nut! But as Arsenal like to keep the ball on the ground, it doesn't really matter that much!

PENALTIES!

9 7

With a 100 per cent record from the spot at the end of 2002-03, Ruud is as deadly from 12 yards as he is from one! It seems like he doesn't feel the massive pressure of penalties, and bagged more spot-kicks than any other Premiership striker last season!

Henry may not have been the first-choice penalty-taker at Arsenal, but only because Dennis Bergkamp's had the job for so long! The Frenchman doesn't disappoint from the spot and there's no doubt he's got the cool, calm composure to take spot-kicks!

FINISHING!

9 9

Unlike former Man. United striker Andy Cole, Ruud doesn't need five chances to score – a half-chance will do! He's been the Champions League's top scorer for the past two seasons and set a new Premiership record last season by scoring in nine league games in a row!

One of Henry's biggest qualities is his ability to score from inside or outside the box and with either foot. His record of roughly one goal every two games speaks for itself and confirms his position as one of the most deadly finishers in the game! Nuff respect!

TEAMWORK!

7 9

Although very single-minded in his quest for goals, Van Nistelrooy does a lot of unselfish work for the team which often gets ignored. He's the perfect target man who can hold on to the ball long enough to bring his United team-mates into play and create chances!

What makes Henry such an unbelievable player is that he often makes just as many goals as he scores – which is as good as scoring them himself. Strike partners Dennis Bergkamp and Francis Jeffers must relish playing alongside Henry with his creative flair!

POTENTIAL!

8 9

At just 27 years of age, Van Nistelrooy still has a good few years left at the highest level if he can stay fit and injury-free. It may sound unbelievable, but the Dutch hitman hasn't even reached his peak – a scary thought for any defender! Watch out for the future!

Thierry is a year younger than Ruud, and just like the Man. United striker, he's only going to get better. Think how good his goal record will be in ten years' time! There's no doubting it, Henry will become one of the greatest ever strikers in the next few years, wait and see!

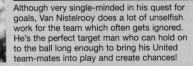

VERDICT

66   **67**

These guys are two of the hottest strikers in the world, and defenders wet their pants just thinking about them! It's almost impossible to decide between them, but Henry's superior pace, skill and ability to create a goal out of nothing just tips the scales in his favour! But for both players will only improve, and seeing these two fight it out for the Golden Boot in the next few years will be breathtaking stuff!

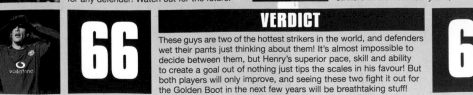

"You can... quote me on that"
THE BEST OF 2003!

"We played without really running most of the time, just passing the ball around and saving our energy."
Sir Alex Ferguson makes sure he doesn't miss the opportunity to wind up big rivals Liverpool after Man. United's emphatic 4-0 win over The Reds!

"I shouldn't really say what I feel, but Poll was their best midfielder. You saw him coming off at half-time and he smiled so much, he obviously enjoyed that performance."
Sheffield United boss Neil Warnock isn't the happiest chappie in the world after ref Graham Poll plays a hand in Arsenal's winner against The Blades in the 2003 FA Cup semi-final.

"I cannae ever sell him because the other players' wives, the manager's wife and the coach's wife will all be up in arms!"
Southampton manager Gordon Strachan says he can't ever sell goal machine James Beattie, who apparently is a hit with the ladies! So not just because he scores loads on the pitch then, Gordon? Duh!

"If Luis Enrique was a girl then I'd marry him."
Former Spain gaffer Javier Clemente reveals his love for Barcelona pretty boy Luis Enrique, and probably scares the pants off poor little Luis along the way!

"Playing against English clubs is like when your mother forced you to eat vegetables when you didn't like it. You have to suffer a bit if you want to be strong."
Inter Milan striker Hernan Crespo does his best to show just how much he loves the English game. We think you should shut up and eat your greens, son!

MATCH

Thierry Henry ★ France

WORLD SUPERSTARS

WORLD SUPER STRIKERS!

WAYNE ROONEY

Wayne Rooney timeline...

October
BABY ROONEY
Wayne is born in the same year that Everton win the league title.

1985

April
ON THE TERRACES
Baby Rooney is carried to his first game at Goodison Park.

1986

FOOTY MAD
Makes his debut for the Western Approaches Under-11 team, aged seven.

1992

May
GOAL FEST
Smashes the Liverpool Schools Under-11 goalscoring record.

1993

MORE GOALS
Scores 99 goals for the Everton Academy's Under-10 team.

1994

November
MASCOT FUN
Wayne is the mascot for heroes Everton in the Merseyside derby.

1996

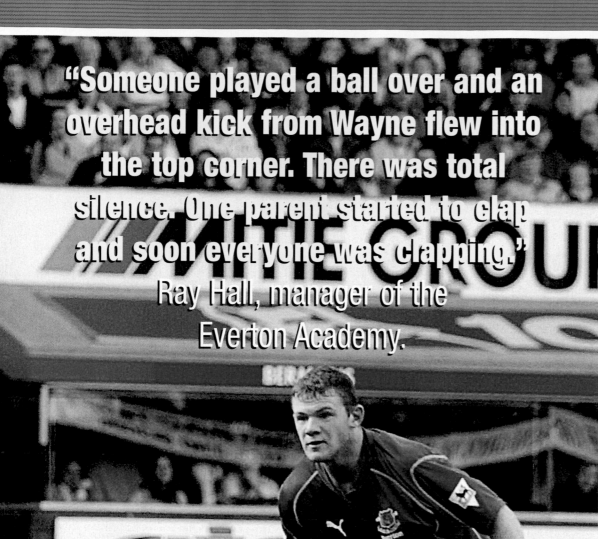

"Someone played a ball over and an overhead kick from Wayne flew into the top corner. There was total silence. One parent started to clap and soon everyone was clapping." Ray Hall, manager of the Everton Academy.

MATCH charts the rapid rise of EVERTON star WAYNE ROONEY!

Wayne Rooney's story puts a smile on the face of any football fan. The tale of a lad who leapt from booting a ball around the streets of Liverpool to playing for England in a matter of months is the stuff of dreams. But for wonder kid Wayne Rooney, the dream has become reality!

So how do we know 'Roonaldo' is the real thing and not just some other young 'star' who's going to disappear in a few years? Well, his first league goal was a Goal Of The Season contender, he smashed the 30-game unbeaten record of Premiership champions Arsenal last season, and Arsene Wenger has called him the best talent he's ever seen in England. So it's safe to say Wayne Rooney might be just a little bit special!

Twelve months ago, Rooney was Everton's best-kept secret. But after a whirlwind debut season, everyone from Ronaldo to Pele, and from David Beckham to Robbie Williams, were drooling over his ability. So in honour of the boy who made his dreams come true, MATCH traces the lightning progress of England's new star Wayne Rooney – from the terraces to the turf of Goodison Park!

CAREER FACTFILE

Born: October 24, 1985 in Liverpool
Nationality: English
Position: Striker
Height: 5ft 10ins
Weight: 12st 4lbs
Former clubs: None
Signed: From Trainee on April 20, 2002
Everton debut: August 17, 2002 v Spurs
Total Everton games/goals: 37/ 8 (August 2002 to July 2003)
International caps/goals: 5/0 (February 2003 to June 2003)

YOUTH CUP HERO
Scores eight goals in eight games for Everton on their way to FA Youth Cup final.

2001

August

PREMIERSHIP DEBUT
Makes his debut against Tottenham in a 2-2 draw at Goodison Park.

October

WORTHY WINNER
Scores twice against Wrexham in the Worthington Cup to become Everton's youngest ever scorer.

THAT GOAL
Becomes the youngest Premiership goalscorer ever with a 30-yard strike against Arsenal.

2002

November

GOAL GRABBER
Scores the only goal as Everton beat Leeds at Elland Road for the first time in over 50 years.

December

MERSEY MAYHEM
Comes on as a sub and hits the bar in his first Merseyside derby at Anfield.

BAD BOY
Against Birmingham, becomes the youngest ever Premiership player to be be sent off.

TROPHY-TASTIC
Wins BBC Young Sports Personality Of the Year Award.

2003

January

TOFFEES DEAL
Signs a three-year deal with Everton.

February

SVEN CALLS
Becomes youngest ever England player against Australia.

April

NATIONAL HERO
Starts first competitive England game against Turkey and gets Man Of The Match Award.

VILLA THRILLER
Scores a last-minute winner as Everton beat Aston Villa 2-1 in the Premiership.

June

ENGLAND REGULAR
Keeps place for Euro 2004 qualifier against Slovakia.

August

WAYNE'S WORLD
Gets ready for the 2003-04 season!

1985

MEET THE ROONEYS!

Wayne Rooney was born on October 24, 1985 in Croxteth, Liverpool – just a mile from Everton FC's Bellefield training ground. His father, also called Wayne, is a former boxer and his mother Jeanette is a school dinner lady. But his whole family are passionate Everton season ticket holders! Wayne was taken to his first game at Goodison Park when he was just six months old, and soon after learning to walk he showed a natural gift for football. The young 'Roonaldo' used to play footy in the streets outside his house with his two younger brothers, Graham and John, and all three ended up at the Everton Youth Academy. But Wayne was the first Rooney to wow the Merseyside scouts!

1993

BOY WONDER!

Wayne had a natural talent for football, but he still used to rush home from school on his BMX to practise his skills. He played his first serious match for an Under-11 team from the Western Approaches pub when he was seven years old, coming on as a sub and scoring! He was soon snapped up by the Liverpool Schools Under-11 side, where he smashed their goalscoring record with over 80 goals in one season! With his strong physique, close ball skills and eye for goal, it wasn't long before professional clubs were trying to sign him, and England youth honours also came his way! If the rumours are true and Wayne Rooney does eat sausage and beans every night, every player should give it a try!

2002

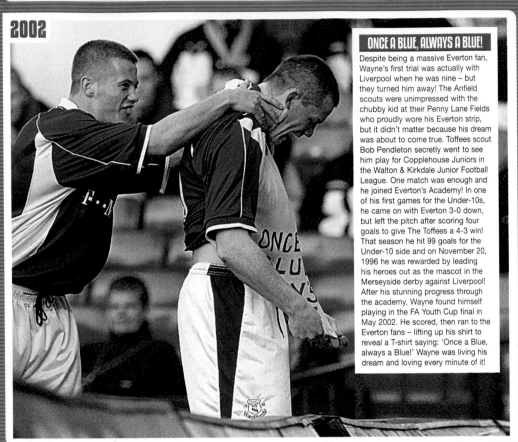

ONCE A BLUE, ALWAYS A BLUE!

Despite being a massive Everton fan, Wayne's first trial was actually with Liverpool when he was nine – but they turned him away! The Anfield scouts were unimpressed with the chubby kid at their Penny Lane Fields who proudly wore his Everton strip, but it didn't matter because his dream was about to come true. Toffees scout Bob Pendleton secretly went to see him play for Copplehouse Juniors in the Walton & Kirkdale Junior Football League. One match was enough and he joined Everton's Academy! In one of his first games for the Under-10s, he came on with Everton 3-0 down, but left the pitch after scoring four goals to give The Toffees a 4-3 win! That season he hit 99 goals for the Under-10 side and on November 20, 1996 he was rewarded by leading his heroes out as the mascot in the Merseyside derby against Liverpool! After his stunning progress through the academy, Wayne found himself playing in the FA Youth Cup final in May 2002. He scored, then ran to the Everton fans – lifting up his shirt to reveal a T-shirt saying: 'Once a Blue, always a Blue!' Wayne was living his dream and loving every minute of it!

2002

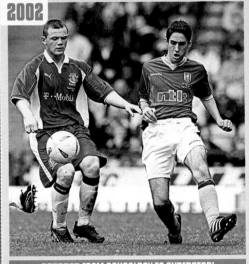

OCTOBER FROM SCHOOLBOY TO SUPERSTAR!

Rooney's rise from the ranks at the Everton Academy to the dizzy heights of the Premiership was nothing short of phenomenal. In contrast to other top players, he completely skipped the reserve team, leaping from the youth team to the first team – and from leaving school at 16 to playing in the Premiership in a matter of months! Toffees fans started to get excited when the young striker bagged two hat-tricks during pre-season in 2002, and they went mental when the same 16-year-old scored two goals in a Worthington Cup tie against Wrexham on October 1, 2002! By doing that, he smashed Tommy Lawton's 65-year-old record as Everton's youngest ever goalscorer. The Rooney bandwagon was up and running!

2002

OCTOBER THAT GOAL AGAINST ARSENAL!

Wayne made his Premiership debut in Everton's 2-2 draw with Spurs on August 17, 2002 – but it was his first goal in the Premiership that really announced his arrival. When Everton met Arsenal at Goodison Park on October 19, Arsenal hadn't lost for 30 games and Arsene Wenger claimed his side could go the whole season unbeaten. Rooney had other plans – with the score at 1-1 in the final minute, he hammered a shot past David Seaman which thundered into the net off the underside of the bar. With one strike, he replaced Michael Owen as the Premiership's youngest ever scorer – aged just 16 years and 360 days. Later that evening, Wayne was reportedly spotted out in Liverpool playing footy in the street with his mates!

2002

WAYNE'S WORLD!

In his debut Premiership season, Roonaldo scored six goals and smashed loads more records! His goal against Leeds United on November 3, 2002 gave Everton their first win at Elland Road in over 50 years of trying. He was on the scoresheet again against Blackburn in December, then became the youngest player to be sent off in the Premiership after a mistimed tackle against Birmingham on Boxing Day. Wayne admitted that the best defender he had ever played against was Sol Campbell, but he still scored another goal past Arsenal in March 2003! He also scored against Newcastle in Everton's 2-1 win in April, before hitting a last-minute winner against Aston Villa on April 26, when everyone was saying he was tired after a long season! In December, Roonaldo won the BBC Young Sports Personality Of The Year Award, then finished runner-up for both the 2003 PFA Young Player Of The Year Award and the 2003 World Newcomer Award at the Sporting Oscars!

2003

FEBRUARY ENGLAND STAR!

Before he had even started ten games for Everton, Wayne came on as a sub in England's friendly with Australia in February 2003 to become England's youngest ever player – aged just 17 years and 111 days! The big question was, would Sven pick him again for the crucial Euro 2004 qualifier with Turkey soon after? The Swede was undecided, but something happened in training that made up his mind. Rooney started by juggling the ball at his feet, then sped off past three players and chipped David Seaman from 30 yards. The whole team stared in stunned silence. Then David Beckham started clapping and soon everyone was applauding! Sven's mind was made up, and Rooney played against Turkey!

2003

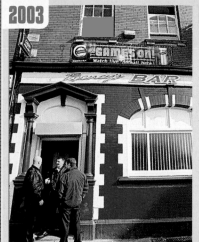

ROONEY-MANIA!

Following his dramatic arrival on the football stage, the whole world started to go Rooney loony! Even while he was still in Everton's youth team, Toffees fanzines had been making predictions about their new Messiah – the one player who could catapult The Toffees back into the big time, in a new era under boss David Moyes. He was born in 1985 – Everton's most successful season in living memory, when they won the league and Cup Winners' Cup – which was spooky, but a good omen for Everton fans! Nicknamed 'The Duke', he was so popular that the Everton website almost crashed when he did his first interview on the net – over 6,000 e-mails arrived in five days! After his England debut, the demand for 'Rooney 9' shirts meant sports stores across the country ran out of the letter 'Y'! He's even had the likes of Ronaldo and Pele queuing up to shower him with praise!

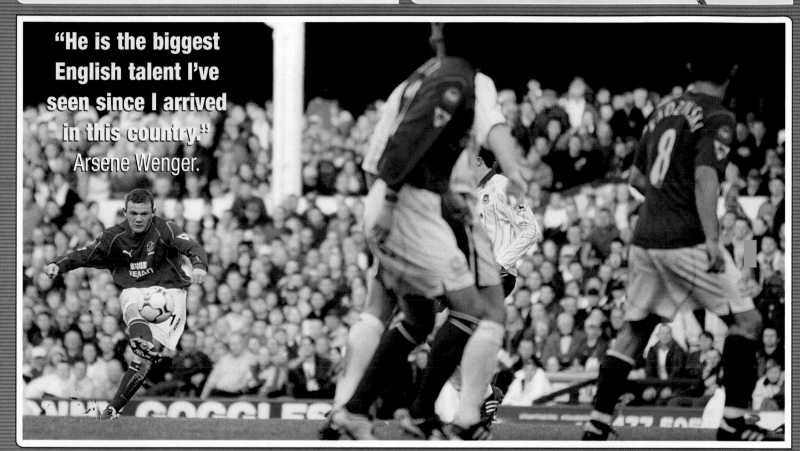

"He is the biggest English talent I've seen since I arrived in this country." Arsene Wenger.

2003

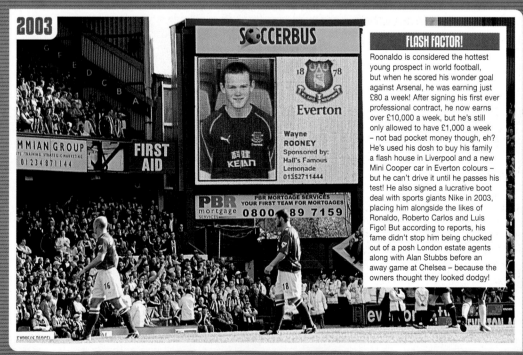

FLASH FACTOR!

Roonaldo is considered the hottest young prospect in world football, but when he scored his wonder goal against Arsenal, he was earning just £80 a week! After signing his first ever professional contract, he now earns over £10,000 a week, but he's still only allowed to have £1,000 a week – not bad pocket money though, eh? He's used his dosh to buy his family a flash house in Liverpool and a new Mini Cooper car in Everton colours – but he can't drive it until he passes his test! He also signed a lucrative boot deal with sports giants Nike in 2003, placing him alongside the likes of Ronaldo, Roberto Carlos and Luis Figo! But according to reports, his fame didn't stop him being chucked out of a posh London estate agents along with Alan Stubbs before an away game at Chelsea – because the owners thought they looked dodgy!

2003

THE FUTURE'S BRIGHT, THE FUTURE'S BLUE!

Wayne ended the 2002-03 season exhausted – but happy! He was already loved by the Everton fans and established himself in the England first-team before he'd turned 18! Things are looking pretty good off the pitch, too. Nike have already registered the name 'Street Striker' in anticipation of his own new brand of boots. But beware, because Everton fans are already looking forward to Rooney II, as Roonaldo's little brother John is currently a promising midfielder in the Everton youth team! The next few years are sure to be great times for Rooney, both with Everton and England. And the future? Any clubs hoping to steal him away from The Toffees should remember one thing – once a Blue, always a Blue!

AC Milan celebrate their 2003 Champions League final victory.

first XI

AC Milan are da current European Champions, but how much do ya know about da Italians?

1 In what year were AC Milan formed – was it 1899 or 1929?

2 True or false? Milan actually used to be a cricket club before switching to football.

3 Who scored the winning penalty in AC Milan's 2003 Champions League final victory?

4 How many times have Milan won the European Cup in their history – is it four, six or eight?

5 Italy international Alessandro Nesta joined Milan in 2002 from which other Italian club – Lazio or Roma?

6 Milan share their amazing 80,000 San Siro stadium with which rival team?

7 Which brilliant France midfielder did AC Milan sell to Arsenal in 1996?

8 Which AC Milan player holds the record for the most appearances made in European competition by an Italian player?

9 Which former Milan ace used to be the manager of both Newcastle and Chelsea in the 1990s?

10 Which president of AC Milan is also the current Italian Prime Minister?

11 True or false? Bobby Robson used to manage Milan back in the 1980s.

1 POINT PER CORRECT ANSWER

WORDFIT

Try to fit these flash 'keepers into the grid below! Go on, 'ave a go, son!

CASILLAS

BARTHEZ
BUFFON
CANIZARES
CASILLAS
CUDICINI
DIDA
FRIEDEL
GIVEN
HISLOP
JAASKELAINEN
JAMES
KAHN
KIRKLAND
MARCOS
NIEMI
ROBINSON
SEAMAN
SCHWARZER
TOLDO
WRIGHT

1 POINT PER CORRECT ANSWER (MAXIMUM 20)

FREAK OR UNIQUE!

True or false?
Holland star Edgar Davids wears these snazzy orange shades just to look cool.

2 POINTS FOR CORRECT ANSWER

KIT KINGS

Which Premiership team used to wear this mingin' kit a few years back?

2 POINTS FOR CORRECT ANSWER

⚽ GROUND FORCE ⚽

In wot European city would ya find this stadium?

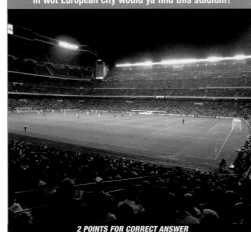

2 POINTS FOR CORRECT ANSWER

THE NICKNAME GAME

See if ya can match these well wicked footy teams with their proper nicknames!

1. England	A. The Azzurri
2. Nigeria	B. Les Bleus
3. Cameroon	C. The Super Eagles
4. Italy	D. The Three Lions
5. France	E. The Indomitable Lions

1 POINT PER CORRECT ANSWER (MAXIMUM 5)

SPELL CHECK STARS

Me naff computer's made a real dog's din-dins outta these Brazil stars' names! Can ya work out who they are to get da points?

1. Junior Knee No
2. Ron Older Dinner
3. Jill Berty Silvia

2 POINTS PER CORRECT ANSWER

CAP IN HAND

How many caps did Gary Lineker win during his ace England career?

a) 70
b) 80
c) 90

2 POINTS FOR CORRECT ANSWER

EYE EYE!

Work out who these five strikers are by peekin' into their mince pies! See if ya can get the full ten points!

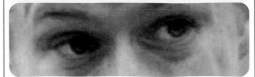

2 POINTS PER CORRECT ANSWER (MAXIMUM 10)

MATCH

WORLD SUPERSTARS

Damien Duff ★ Rep. Of Ireland

WORLD SUPER STRIKERS!

RAUL

Raul timeline...

August

GO ATLETICO
Signs up for the Atletico Madrid youth team, fulfilling his boyhood dreams.

1990

July

REAL SWITCH
Switches to Real Madrid after Atletico get rid of their youth team.

1993

October

DEBUT BOY
Makes his debut against Real Zaragoza aged 17 and scores in his next game – against Atletico Madrid in a 3-2 win!

1994

May

MAKING WAVES
Finishes his first season for Real with nine goals from 28 games.

1995

May

SPAIN PAIN
Finishes the season with 19 goals from 40 games and is Real's top scorer, but he is left out of Spain's Euro '96 squad.

1996

May

TOP MAN
Finishes as La Liga's top scorer with 21 goals for the Bernabeu giants.

1997

> ## "Real bought Figo, Zidane and Ronaldo – but the best player in the world at the moment is Raul."
> ### Sir Alex Ferguson.

***MATCH** charts the rapid rise of **REAL MADRID** star **RAUL**!*

When Sir Alex Ferguson says you're the world's best player, you know you're on to a good thing! But Raul doesn't need to be told he's one of football's true megastars!

At 26, he is the most powerful player at the world's most powerful club. The Real Madrid striker has complete control over a dressing room of stars like Zidane, Ronaldo, Carlos and Beckham, and he's said to be bigger than the club president! But how did a young Atletico Madrid fan become the prince of football's aristocrats?

You have to look first at Raul's amazing ability. After breaking into the Real team at 17, he was soon hammering in goals as the club rose from being an average side to the all-star line-up you see today. He's not that quick, he hasn't got a great right foot and he isn't brilliant in the air. But with a better footy brain than anyone else, he's a record goalscorer and a master creator for his team-mates.

With three European Cups, four league titles, and countless other trophies under his belt, Raul is already a living legend. MATCH reveals how he's become the Crown Prince of Real Madrid!

CAREER FACTFILE

Born: June 27, 1977 in Madrid

Nationality: Spanish

Position: Striker

Height: 5ft 10ins

Weight: 11st 4lbs

Former clubs: Atletico Madrid

Signed: From trainee, June 1992

Real Madrid debut: v Real Zaragoza, October 29, 1994

Total Real Madrid games/goals: 330/163 (October 1994 to July 2003)

International caps/goals: Spain 65/33 (October 1996 to July 2003)

May
EURO JOY
Plays 89 minutes in midfield as Real Madrid win the European Cup, beating Juventus 1-0 in the final.

1998

March
GOAL CRAZY
Scores seven goals in four days for Spain, hitting four in a 9-0 win over Austria and three against San Marino!

1999

April
UNITED BEATEN
Scores twice as Real beat Man. United 3-2 to knock the holders out of the Champs League.

May
SECOND CUP WIN
Lifts the European Cup with a win over Valencia, scoring a brilliant third goal in the final.

June
EURO OUT
Heartbreak for Raul as his late penalty miss against France in the Euro 2000 quarter-final sees Spain crash out.

2000

March
HANDFUL
Admits he deliberately handballed a goal against Leeds to give Real a 3-2 win in the Champs League!

November
MEDAL MANIA
Comes third in the World Player Of The Year and second in the European Player Of The Year awards.
2001

May
THIRD EUROPEAN CUP WIN
Scores in the 2002 Champions League final as Real Madrid beat Bayer Leverkusen.

June
CUP DOUBLE
Scores twice against South Africa at the 2002 World Cup but is injured against the Republic Of Ireland.
2002

April
QUARTER CRACKER
Scores two crackers as Real beat Man. United 3-1 in the Champions League quarter-final.
2003

May
SEMI PAIN
Crashes out of the Champions League after Juventus beat Real in the semi-finals.

June
TITLE TRIUMPH
Wins the Spanish title for Real with two goals in a 4-0 victory over city rivals Atletico.

1992

ATLETICO BOY!

As a boy, Raul was a massive Atletico Madrid fan and was delighted to sign for his local team. Atletico were the working man's club in town – while Real Madrid were seen as the club of the rich and the powerful. Having come from the poorer side of town, the young prodigy was proud to have joined his boyhood idols. But it all went wrong when Atletico president Jesus Gil decided that running youth teams was a complete waste of money, and got rid of them in 1992. A young Raul was absolutely devastated, so with no other club to play for, he joined rivals Real Madrid in a decision that he's never regretted. When Raul went on to become a massive world star, it was Jesus Gil of rivals Atletico who was regretting his decision!

1994

DEBUT DILEMMA!

Raul was soon seen as the next big star in Spain, and it wasn't long before the striker was being groomed as the hottest young player at The Bernabeu. After scoring a shedload of goals in Real Madrid's youth teams, he finally got his chance in the first team at the age of 17 – at the start of the 1994-95 season. Raul made his long-awaited debut for the men in white against Real Zaragoza. He had a bit of a nightmare in that game, missing three sitters. But the 17-year-old looked unfazed by the big occasion, and when coach Jorge Valdano stuck with him for the next match, Raul repaid his faith with interest! He scored an absolute screamer from the edge of the box, then won a penalty and set up the winner as Real beat their city rivals – and Raul's fave club – Atletico Madrid 3-2 in a cracker of a game!

1998

MAY EURO WINNER!

Real Madrid weren't considered one of the better teams at the start of the 1998 Champions League, but Raul helped them to reach the final against the odds. In the final itself, he was played in midfield and featured for 89 minutes as his side took on hot favourites and European cup holders Juventus. In the 67th minute, Predrag Mijatovic scored the only goal of the game and a 21-year-old Raul began his great relationship with the European Cup with his first ever win! He would go on to become the tournament's record goalscorer.

1998

JUNE WORLD CHUMP!

As usual, Spain went into the 1998 World Cup as everyone's dark horses and an outside bet to win the trophy. The Spanish national team has a reputation for always failing to live up to expectations – despite having some top stars. Raul was seen as the player who could make a real difference for the under-achievers at France '98. But even with his impressive club form during the 1997-98 season, he still couldn't make an impact for his country. He scored a fantastic volley against Nigeria, but Spain lost that thrilling match 3-2 and they crashed out of the tournament at the first stage. Unfortunately, the 1998 World Cup wouldn't be the last time the Real star would suffer international heartache!

2000

MAY FINAL FANTASY!

After seeing off Man. United in the quarter-finals of the 2000 Champions League – thanks to two goals in two minutes at Old Trafford – Raul went into the final with the expectation of all the Real supporters behind him. But he didn't disappoint against an ultra-tough Valencia side, and after goals from Fernando Morientes and Steve McManaman, the Crown Prince notched a brilliant third when he ran half the length of the pitch to round the goalkeeper and coolly slot home! That made it 3-0, and gave Raul his second Champions League medal!

2000

JUNE EURO HEARTBREAK!

Raul went into the 2002 Euro Championships in Holland and Belgium as Spain's golden boy. But as usual, his country made hard work of the tournament – just scraping through the group stages after losing to Norway before beating Slovenia and Yugoslavia. In the quarter-finals, Spain came up against world champions France and gave as good as they got in a pulsating clash. With the score at 2-1 to France in the dying seconds, Spain were awarded a dramatic penalty. Raul stepped up to take responsibility, but with the whole crowd holding their breath in anticipation, he smashed his shot over the bar and Spain went crashing out of the competition. The 23-year-old's pain was there for millions to see!

2001

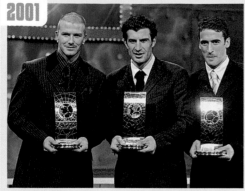

NEARLY MAN!

It seems crazy that as the Champions League's top scorer of all time, a three-times Champions League winner, a five-times league winner, and Spain's record goalscorer, Raul hasn't won any personal awards – but it's true! He came closest in 2001, when he came third in the FIFA World Player Of The Year awards, finishing behind winner and Real Madrid team-mate Luis Figo, and future team-mate David Beckham. "I am very proud to win this award alongside these two excellent footballers," said Raul, collecting his prize at the ceremony. "I hope I can go on enjoying football as much as I have done so far." In the European Player Of The Year awards, he came even closer, being beaten only by Michael Owen. But you can bet he's got his eyes on the top trophies – and what Raul wants, he usually gets!

2002

MAY EL MATADOR!

With the mighty Real Madrid now the biggest force in European footy, Champions League failure wasn't an option. But with Figo, Zidane, Carlos and Raul in the ranks, they never had to worry! In 2002, Real reached the final at Hampden Park to face tough German side Bayer Leverkusen, but Raul put his side 1-0 ahead thanks to an error from defender Lucio. Lucio scored an equaliser himself, but a sensational Zidane volley settled the match and Raul collected his third European Cup! As his team-mates began celebrating, Raul waved a huge Spanish flag as though he was a native bullfighter taunting a raging bull! Real then went on to win the European Super Cup, beating the reigning UEFA Cup winners Feyenoord 3-1, before defeating Olympia de Asuncion 2-0 in the Inter-Continental Cup. Real could finally claim to be the best team in the world!

"He is one of the most influential figures in the team on and off the field. The amazing thing is he's still only 26."
Steve McManaman.

2002

JUNE WORLD HEARTBREAK!

After heartbreak at France '98 and Euro 2000, Raul was hoping for a change of fortunes at the 2002 World Cup in South Korea & Japan. Spain started well, with Raul scoring twice against South Africa as they made it through the group stages easily. But just as things had started to go well for the 25-year-old, he picked up an injury against the Republic Of Ireland in the second round and could only look on as his side scraped past Mick McCarthy's men on penalties. It was a race against time to make the the quarter-final against co-hosts South Korea, but Raul didn't make it, and he had to sit on the sidelines in anguish as his team went out on penalties. It was international pain yet again!

2003

JUNE THE KING OF SPAIN!

By 2003, Raul's power at Real Madrid had reached a point where he was considered more powerful than the coach or the club president! This was tested when Ronaldo joined the club and he was publicly critical of the World Player Of The Year. The side stuttered as Ronaldo struggled, but with pressure from Raul, the Brazil star bucked up his ideas and things improved. They reached a high point as Real – with two classy goals from Raul – wiped the floor with Man. United in a 3-1 Champions League quarter-final victory in Spain. But there would be no Champions League final glory this time, as Juventus knocked them out in the semis. But Raul, and Real of course, will be back!

THE DOs & DON'Ts OF ENGLAND TRAINING!

YOU'RE A CUTE LITTLE FELLA, AREN'T YA?

DO! Be nice to our new hero Wayne Rooney!

DON'T! Forget it's footy you're playing!

SHAQ ATTACK!

GRRR!

UUGGGH!

DO! Try to push your team-mates around!

PARP!

PEEYEW!

DON'T! Eat loads of beans beforehand!

DON'T KNOW, BUT I BET IT'S FUNNY. ER...

WHY DID THE CHICKEN CROSS THE ROAD?

DO! Laugh loudly at Michael Owen's jokes!

DON'T! Forget that strange old man is Tord Grip!

I'M TORD GRIP, I AM - AT LEAST I THINK I AM. WHO AM I?

YES BOSS!

SVEN SAYS... PUT YOUR HANDS UNDER YOUR ARMPITS!

DO! Copy what Sven does at all times!

EH UP LADS, HAVE I MISSED ANYTHING?

DON'T! Turn up for training half an hour late!

DO! Join in with all the silly dances - they're fun!

WE ARE THE CHEEKY GIRLS, YOU ARE THE CHEEKY BOYS!

EEEK! I'M STUCK, LA!

DON'T! Put superglue on your training tops. Doh!

WHERE'S ME PEGS, LA?

DO! Put up your own tent on arrival!

EEH LOOK - THERE'S WESTLIFE!

DON'T! Run around like a girl!

ICELAND FOOTY RESULTS!

MATCH exclusively brings you all the latest scores from the fun and friendly Icelandic league!

England
Iceland

Gudfellas Pizza **0-0** Mi Crochips

Kaptain Burdsye **3-1** Crispi Pankakes

Froze Npees **2-2** Haa Gandaas

Potato Waffals **1-0** Findus Lassangna

Fishfingas **0-1** Norfsee Prorns

Burgas **1-1** Lamchops

Mumsgon **2-0** Eysland

Garlik Keyev **0-3** Garlik Bred

RUSTU'S FACE PAINT SECRET!

Ever wondered why Turkey goalkeeper Rustu Recber wears face paint? Well despite what some people think, it's not to scare the opposition to death – it's to keep the glare of the stadium lights out of his eyes during the match. Bless him!

"I never use paint to achieve a certain look," explained the crazy stopper. **"The stadium lights dazzle me, so I use the paint to stop the glare. I used it more in the World Cup because I had an allergic reaction to the pitch and conditions!"**

So there you have it. And there we were thinking he was just a bit pants at putting on his make-up – you live and learn, eh?

MATCH

David Beckham ★ England

WORLD SUPERSTARS

PERFECT MORNING?

"I'd like to wake up somewhere in America. I'd say somewhere nice and hot like Miami or California. I'd get up at around 11.30am after a nice little lie-in! I usually get up at 8.45am when we've got training at Newcastle, so it would make a nice change to stay in bed!"

PERFECT TUNES?

"I'm listening to a lot of Tupac's music at the moment – I love Tupac! And Jay-Z as well, he's really hot. Who else? I've got Fabolous on my car stereo – a rapper I like – but maybe I'd slow it down a bit with some Maxwell!"

PERFECT AFTERNOON?

"Well I wouldn't go to training on my perfect afternoon! I'd probably go into town to do some shopping and buy myself some nice clothes. Newcastle has some nice shops, but I'd prefer to go to London. Hopefully it would be nice and hot, so I could just go and chill in a bar somewhere with a few of the lads."

PERFECT MOTOR?

"That's a tough one! I think I'd have to say a Ferrari Spider convertible. I've never driven a Ferrari before, but I think they're a brilliant car. They look great and I'd love to have one eventually. I've got a BMW X5 now which I love, but you can't beat a Ferrari!"

PERFECT BREAKFAST?

"I'd have a nice fry-up! I know it's not particularly healthy, but I can have them for breakfast whenever I want because I'm naturally quite slim. Yeah, a nice big fry-up after a long lie-in!"

PERFECT DATE?

"I'm a big fan of Christina Milian actually! She's a pop singer, but she's also done some presenting on MTV as well. I like her a lot!"

Jermaine Jenas's...
Perfect day!

*How would **JERMAINE JENAS** spend his perfect 24 hours? The **NEWCASTLE** & **ENGLAND** star tells **MATCH** it would be made up of wicked tunes, flash cars, holidays and more!*

PERFECT HOLIDAY?

"My perfect holiday destination would have to be Los Angeles in America and I'd go and watch the LA Lakers play basketball. I haven't been to LA before but it's definitely in my plans to go and watch a Lakers game when I get the chance. I like watching basketball, but I don't play."

PERFECT MEAL?

"There's a pasta dish they make up in Newcastle called Penne Arrabiata, and for me there's nothing better! It's pasta with prawns in a spicy chilli sauce, and if I could eat that all the time I think I probably would!"

PERFECT SIGNING?

"I was well happy when I heard rumours that Rivaldo might sign for Newcastle earlier last season because I think he's a fantastic player. But if I had to choose my ideal signing, I'd say Ronaldo. I'd love to hear that Ronaldo was coming to Newcastle so I could play alongside him!"

PERFECT MATCH?

"It would have to be the World Cup final – there's no bigger game than that in football, is there? To be there watching two great teams play, like Argentina and Brazil, would be amazing. The rivalry those two have, and in a World Cup final, would be something else and I'd love to see it!"

"I'd love to hear that Ronaldo was coming to Newcastle so I could play alongside him!"

CAPTION CRAZY!

MATCH loves having a laugh at the world of footy – take a look at some of this year's wicked pictures!

Graeme Souness can't believe Gary Megson's mouth really IS that big!

SO AWAY LITTLE BOY, IT'S BED TIME FOR YOU!

HELP ME, MY PARACHUTE HASN'T OPENED!

SHOOT! SHOOT!

IT'S NOT EVEN KICKED OFF YET, MUM!

BUT YOU SAID PLAY A FLAT BACK FOUR, GAFFER!

NO ORANGES AT HALF-TIME? RIGHT, THAT'S IT!

Robbie Keane hears that the Tottenham treatment room is full again.

SET OFF ME! I'M NOT THE WEST HAM MASCOT, YOU KNOW!

WARM UP WITH ME, LADS... AND STRETCH, EVERYBODY!

NOW WHERE DID I PUT MY CAR KEYS AGAIN?

GET IN, MUM'S DOING CHIPS FOR TEA TONIGHT!

Paolo di Canio waterlogs the West Ham pitch!

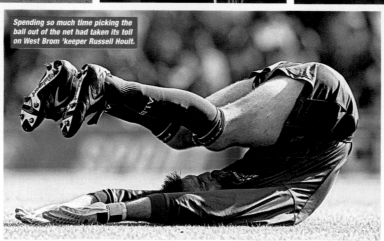

Spending so much time picking the ball out of the net had taken its toll on West Brom 'keeper Russell Hoult.

WELL, THEY SAID EVERTON WERE FLYING HIGH!

MATCH

WORLD SUPERSTARS

Ruud van Nistelrooy ★ Holland

WHAT HAPPEN

JOE COLE

TOP TEEN RANKING IN 2000: 1 AGE NOW: 21

WHAT DID WE SAY THEN? That Joe was the most exciting talent in English football! The tricky midfielder had already been West Ham's worst kept secret for a few years, and made his debut just after his 17th birthday. We said sublime skill would take him right to the top.

WHAT DO WE SAY NOW? Joe still has time to take the Premiership and the England team by storm. But he's already made an impact for both, wearing the captain's armband for West Ham and scoring his first goal for England in June. Relegation was a blow, but Joe Cole will be back!

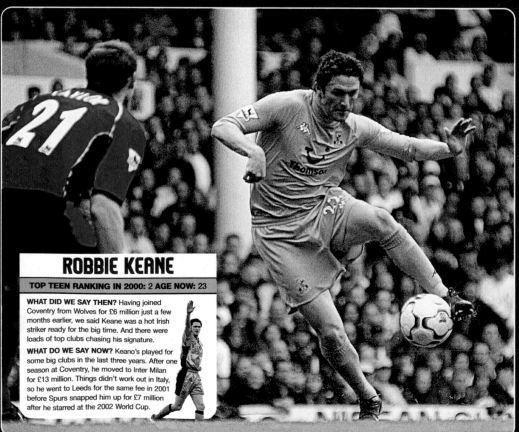

ROBBIE KEANE

TOP TEEN RANKING IN 2000: 2 AGE NOW: 23

WHAT DID WE SAY THEN? Having joined Coventry from Wolves for £6 million just a few months earlier, we said Keane was a hot Irish striker ready for the big time. And there were loads of top clubs chasing his signature.

WHAT DO WE SAY NOW? Keano's played for some big clubs in the last three years. After one season at Coventry, he moved to Inter Milan for £13 million. Things didn't work out in Italy, so he went to Leeds for the same fee in 2001 before Spurs snapped him up for £7 million after he starred at the 2002 World Cup.

STEVEN GERRARD

TOP TEEN RANKING IN 2000: 3 AGE NOW: 23

WHAT DID WE SAY THEN? Liverpool lad Gerrard had enjoyed a breakthrough season for The Reds in 2000. The versatile youngster had played in several positions for the first team and he looked mature beyond his teenage years. MATCH reckoned his first senior England caps were just around the corner!

WHAT DO WE SAY NOW? Stevie G has become a midfield powerhouse for club and country, totally living up to the hype we gave him. He made his England debut just before Euro 2000 and also played in that tournament, though England crashed out early. Gerrard helped Liverpool to three cups in 2001, has starred in the Champions League and is one of the best midfielders around.

ED NEXT?

Back in 2000, **MATCH** featured the 50 teenagers who were ready to set English footy alight! But three years on, who's made it big in the Premiership and who hasn't? Check out our top teen update!

GARETH BARRY

TOP TEEN RANKING IN 2000: 4 AGE NOW: 22

WHAT DID WE SAY THEN? Gareth was busy making the Aston Villa left-back spot his own back in 2000, even at the age of 18. Playing like an experienced pro, the England Under-18 skipper had already joined up with the Under-21 side and had a massive, massive future in Villa's defence.

WHAT DO WE SAY NOW? Barry's still a vital player for Villa and now has full England honours – even though he fell out of favour at Villa under John Gregory and switched positions several times. He looks settled in left midfield now, and after captaining the England Under-21s, he's hoping to become a regular in Sven's senior side.

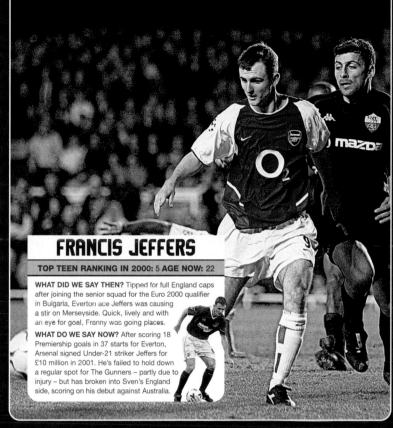

FRANCIS JEFFERS

TOP TEEN RANKING IN 2000: 5 AGE NOW: 22

WHAT DID WE SAY THEN? Tipped for full England caps after joining the senior squad for the Euro 2000 qualifier in Bulgaria, Everton ace Jeffers was causing a stir on Merseyside. Quick, lively and with an eye for goal, Franny was going places.

WHAT DO WE SAY NOW? After scoring 18 Premiership goals in 37 starts for Everton, Arsenal signed Under-21 striker Jeffers for £10 million in 2001. He's failed to hold down a regular spot for The Gunners – partly due to injury – but has broken into Sven's England side, scoring on his debut against Australia.

ALAN SMITH

TOP TEEN RANKING IN 2000: 6 AGE NOW: 23

WHAT DID WE SAY THEN? Smithy had already broken into the Leeds first team and scored on his debut at Liverpool. The striker had already suffered setbacks – like breaking his ankle and coming home from the FA's Lilleshall School – but was on the verge of big things.

WHAT DO WE SAY NOW? Smithy's a big fave with Leeds fans, who love his all-action style. Despite playing in midfield a lot for Leeds, he's made his England debut and scored against Portugal – before getting sent off against Macedonia. His discipline remains a concern.

...AND THE REST!

MATCH looks at the rest of our top 50 teenagers from three years ago to catch up with how they've done!

MARK BURCHILL
TOP TEEN RANKING IN 2000: 9 AGE NOW: 23

What's happened to him? Burchill didn't get a regular game at Celtic, so he moved to Portsmouth in 2001. Has had loan spells at Birmingham, Ipswich and Dundee.

MATTHEW JONES
TOP TEEN RANKING IN 2000: 13 AGE NOW:23

What's happened to him? Jones joined Leicester from Leeds for £3 million in 2000, but several injuries and a loss of form saw him available on a free transfer in 2003.

MICHAEL REDDY
TOP TEEN RANKING IN 2000: 14 AGE NOW: 23

What's happened to him? Reddy hadn't started a league game at Sunderland up to July 2003 but he's been at Swindon, Hull, Barnsley, York and Sheff. Wed. on loan.

CURTIS WOODHOUSE
TOP TEEN RANKING IN 2000: 15 AGE NOW:

What's happened to him? Birmingham signed Curtis for £1 million in 2001 from Sheffield United, but Steve Bruce sent the midfielder on loan to Rotherham in 2003.

LUKE CHADWICK
TOP TEEN RANKING IN 2000: 17 AGE NOW:

What's happened to him? Chances have been slim for Chadwick, who had played in 39 Man. United games by the end of last season. Loaned to Reading and Burnley.

IAN ARMSTRONG
TOP TEEN RANKING IN 2000: 18 AGE NOW: 21

What's happened to him? The England youth striker failed to make a first-team appearance for Liverpool and moved to Port Vale in 2001 in order to get a game.

STEPHEN BYWATER

TOP TEEN RANKING IN 2000: 19 **AGE NOW:** 22

What's happened to him? The goalkeeper had played in five league games for West Ham before relegation last season. He's also had five loan spells at other clubs.

LEON KNIGHT

TOP TEEN RANKING IN 2000: 21 **AGE NOW:** 21

What's happened to him? Striker Knight hasn't broken into Chelsea's first team but he's enjoyed spells on loan at QPR, Huddersfield and Sheffield Wednesday.

TOMMY SMITH

TOP TEEN RANKING IN 2000: 22 **AGE NOW:** 23

What's happened to him? Fast and skilful striker Smith, a former England Under-21 international, had his Watford contract up for renewal in the summer of 2003.

GARY McSHEFFREY

TOP TEEN RANKING IN 2000: 24 **AGE NOW:** 21

What's happened to him? Coventry's youngest-ever player is doing his best to live up to the hype at Highfield Road and hit eight goals from midfield in 2002-03.

LEE MORRIS

TOP TEEN RANKING IN 2000: 26 **AGE NOW:** 23

What's happened to him? The former England Under-21 forward scored nine goals for Derby in 2002-03 but has yet to live up to his £3 million price tag.

ADAM MURRAY

TOP TEEN RANKING IN 2000: 27 **AGE NOW:** 22

What's happened to him? The midfielder had a successful loan spell with Mansfield in 2002, then returned to Derby to play 22 games in Division One last season.

MICHAEL CARRICK

TOP TEEN RANKING IN 2000: 7 **AGE NOW:** 22

WHAT DID WE SAY THEN? Although Joe Cole was getting all the attention at West Ham, Carrick was also being tipped for the big time. The elegant midfielder enjoyed a loan spell at Swindon but wanted to become a Hammers regular.

WHAT DO WE SAY NOW? Carrick's now played over 100 games for West Ham and won full England caps. With his talent, and the clubs that showed an interested in him after West Ham were relegated in 2003, he'll soon be back.

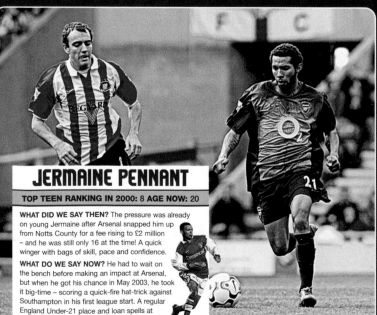

JERMAINE PENNANT

TOP TEEN RANKING IN 2000: 8 **AGE NOW:** 20

WHAT DID WE SAY THEN? The pressure was already on young Jermaine after Arsenal snapped him up from Notts County for a fee rising to £2 million – and he was still only 16 at the time! A quick winger with bags of skill, pace and confidence.

WHAT DO WE SAY NOW? He had to wait on the bench before making an impact at Arsenal, but when he got his chance in May 2003, he took it big-time – scoring a quick-fire hat-trick against Southampton in his first league start. A regular England Under-21 place and loan spells at Watford have shown he's still got a big future.

STUART TAYLOR

TOP TEEN RANKING IN 2000: 10 **AGE NOW:** 22

WHAT DID WE SAY THEN? The promising youngster was said to be challenging David Seaman and Alex Manninger for Arsenal's No.1 jersey, but he knew he'd have to wait for his chance in Arsene Wenger's side with top goalkeepers like that at Highbury. The England Under-18 star hadn't yet made his Arsenal debut in 2000, but he was gearing up for it.

WHAT DO WE SAY NOW? Giant stopper Taylor had made 30 Arsenal appearances by the end of last season, but he's never really challenged for the club's No.1 jersey. A very capable deputy when David Seaman, Richard Wright or Rami Shaaban were injured, he played sufficient games in the 2001-02 campaign to earn a championship medal.

oile · CFC · CHELSEA VICE-PRESIDENTS

JOHN TERRY

TOP TEEN RANKING IN 2000: 11 AGE NOW: 22

WHAT DID WE SAY THEN? Terry had already seen action under manager Gianluca Vialli – playing at centre-back, right-back and in centre-midfield in his first three games for Chelsea! Getting a regular place for The Blues looked promising.

WHAT DO WE SAY NOW? Terry is tipped as a future Chelsea captain and, having won his first and much-overdue England cap in May 2003, he's now a defender that every Premiership club would love to have in their side. His defensive partnership with William Gallas could give The Blues the base they need to challenge for the title.

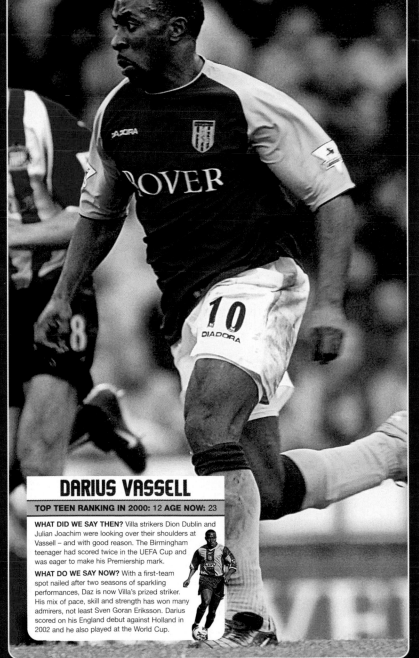

DARIUS VASSELL

TOP TEEN RANKING IN 2000: 12 AGE NOW: 23

WHAT DID WE SAY THEN? Villa strikers Dion Dublin and Julian Joachim were looking over their shoulders at Vassell – and with good reason. The Birmingham teenager had scored twice in the UEFA Cup and was eager to make his Premiership mark.

WHAT DO WE SAY NOW? With a first-team spot nailed after two seasons of sparkling performances, Daz is now Villa's prized striker. His mix of pace, skill and strength has won many admirers, not least Sven Goran Eriksson. Darius scored on his England debut against Holland in 2002 and he also played at the World Cup.

JERMAIN DEFOE

TOP TEEN RANKING IN 2000: 16 AGE NOW: 21

WHAT DID WE SAY THEN? We liked the look of this confident young striker! A graduate from the FA's highly successful Lilleshall School, Defoe had already swapped Charlton for West Ham in a bid to make an impact in the Premiership and was waiting desperately on The Hammers' bench.

WHAT DO WE SAY NOW? A goal-grabbing loan spell at Bournemouth in 2001 shot JD to fame, and he returned to West Ham ready for the big time. He cemented his first-team place last season and scored 11 goals despite relegation.

PAUL KONCHESKY

TOP TEEN RANKING IN 2000: 20 AGE NOW: 22

WHAT DID WE SAY THEN? Not many 17-year-olds get a taste of the Premiership, but left-back Konchesky did that in the 1998-99 season. Charlton's youngest-ever league player was highly rated at The Valley and was being tipped for the top.

WHAT DO WE SAY NOW? We like to feel that Konchesky has proved us right – as he's an established Premiership star from Charlton's youth academy. With plenty of England Under-21 caps behind him, the attacking full-back also won full honours after coming on against Australia in February 2003. Handed in a transfer request at Charlton during the summer.

SHAUN ALLAWAY

TOP TEEN RANKING IN 2000: 28 AGE NOW: 20

What's happened to him? England youth goalkeeper Allaway moved to Leeds from Reading for a £300,000 fee in 2000 and is waiting to make his big breakthrough.

MARVIN BROWN

TOP TEEN RANKING IN 2000: 29 AGE NOW: 20

What's happened to him? Striker Brown had loan spells last season at Torquay and Cheltenham. Still hoping to make a big impression in the Bristol City first team.

ADAM NEWTON

TOP TEEN RANKING IN 2000: 30 AGE NOW: 22

What's happened to him? After two sub appearances for West Ham and spells at Notts County and Leyton Orient, the full-back joined Peterborough in 2002.

DAVID WRIGHT

TOP TEEN RANKING IN 2000: 31 AGE NOW: 23

What's happened to him? The right-back has hardly missed a match over the past four seasons and he's now played over 200 games for First Division Crewe.

IAN STONEBRIDGE

TOP TEEN RANKING IN 2000: 34 AGE NOW: 22

What's happened to him? The former trainee Tottenham striker hasn't yet made it back to the Premiership but is currently starring for Plymouth in Division Two.

LIONEL MORGAN

TOP TEEN RANKING IN 2000: 36 AGE NOW: 20

What's happened to him? The forward remains a talent, even though he doesn't always get a game for Wimbledon and may fancy a move away from the club.

41

CHRIS DOIG
TOP TEEN RANKING IN 2000: 37 **AGE NOW:** 22

What's happened to him? Still something of a bit-part player for Nottingham Forest, the young defender will hope to get more chances in the future for the Midlands club.

DANNY WEBBER
TOP TEEN RANKING IN 2000: 38 **AGE NOW:** 21

What's happened to him? With no games in four seasons at Man. United, striker Webber joined Watford in 2003 after a successful loan spell at Vicarage Road.

RYAN GREEN
TOP TEEN RANKING IN 2000: 39 **AGE NOW:** 22

What's happened to him? He became Wales' youngest ever player at 17, but the full-back's career went sour at Wolves and he was released by Sheffield Wednesday.

GARY CALDWELL
TOP TEEN RANKING IN 2000: 40 **AGE NOW:** 21

What's happened to him? Now a senior Scotland international, centre-back Gary's finding it tough to break into Newcastle's team and has been on loan at Coventry.

BRIAN HOWARD
TOP TEEN RANKING IN 2000: 41 **AGE NOW:** 20

What's happened to him? The England youth striker didn't make the grade with Southampton. He got released in 2002 and joined Swindon after several trials.

JONATHAN BEWERS
TOP TEEN RANKING IN 2000: 42 **AGE NOW:** 21

What's happened to him? The defensive midfielder made just a single substitute appearance for Villa in 2000 and has yet to establish himself beyond the reserves.

DAVID PRUTTON
TOP TEEN RANKING IN 2000: 23 **AGE NOW:** 22

WHAT DID WE SAY THEN? Nottingham Forest were in a poor state a few years back in Division One, but one of their bright lights was David Prutton. A tough box-to-box midfielder who was already catching the eye of several scouts, 'Prutts' was earning himself quite a reputation at The City Ground.

WHAT DO WE SAY NOW? The England Under-21 star had bided his time long enough in Division One, so when Southampton moved for him in January 2003, he jumped at the chance of a £2.5 million switch. He expected to wait for his opportunity to impress, but he soon forced his way into The Saints' side and is eager to prove he can succeed in the Premiership.

WAYNE BRIDGE
TOP TEEN RANKING IN 2000: 25 **AGE NOW:** 23

WHAT DID WE SAY THEN? Little known away from his native Southampton, this energetic left-back had already played over 25 Premiership games for The Saints. A local lad and lifelong fan, it was his dream to play for them, and his performances had already pushed him into the England Under-21 squad.

WHAT DO WE SAY NOW? Now pushing Ashley Cole hard for England's left-back spot, Bridgey has become a top player in the Premiership. He's hardly missed a match in the last four seasons and his ability at such a young age convinced Chelsea to splash out £7 million to secure his services in July 2003.

MATTHEW ETHERINGTON
TOP TEEN RANKING IN 2000: 33 **AGE NOW:** 22

WHAT DID WE SAY THEN? Etherington had only been at Tottenham for a few weeks but he had already played first-team footy. Matty started with Peterborough, making his debut at 15 and winning England youth caps. The exciting left winger had trained with Man. United, but joined Spurs along with Simon Davies in 1999.

WHAT DO WE SAY NOW? It's been tough on Matt, who has the talent but isn't always assured of getting a game in Glenn Hoddle's side. He had a successful loan spell at Bradford, and plenty of clubs would be keen to sign him.

SHAUN WRIGHT-PHILLIPS
TOP TEEN RANKING IN 2000: 32 **AGE NOW:** 21

WHAT DID WE SAY THEN? Famous for having Arsenal legend Ian Wright as a dad, the nippy forward was the talk of City. Having made his debut in August 1999 in the League Cup, his aim was to stay in Joe Royle's squad and push on to make more league appearances and score some goals.

WHAT DO WE SAY NOW? Shaun never really made it as a striker under Royle but when Kevin Keegan came in, the young star was switched to right wing-back and he's become a regular in that position. England Under-21 caps have also come his way since 2000.

LEDLEY KING

TOP TEEN RANKING IN 2000: 35 AGE NOW: 22

WHAT DID WE SAY THEN? When MATCH featured this talented Tottenham centre-back, he'd already been on the bench for an FA Cup semi-final and made his debut at Anfield, so the big occasion didn't faze him. He hadn't won a regular place in the Spurs side, but with strength, speed and aerial ability, it was only a matter of time.

WHAT DO WE SAY NOW? That we were spot on! Now one of the first names on the team-sheet, the blow of losing Sol Campbell to Arsenal was softened when 'King Ledley' stepped into his boots. The defender made his England debut in a friendly against Italy in March 2002, and he'll be keeping strikers quiet for a long time to come.

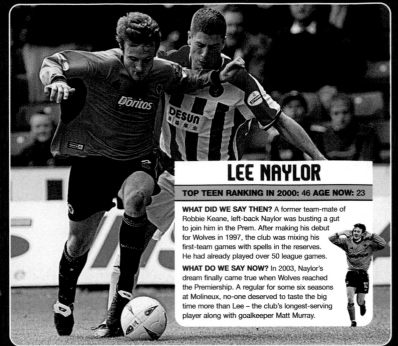

LEE NAYLOR

TOP TEEN RANKING IN 2000: 46 AGE NOW: 23

WHAT DID WE SAY THEN? A former team-mate of Robbie Keane, left-back Naylor was busting a gut to join him in the Prem. After making his debut for Wolves in 1997, the club was mixing his first-team games with spells in the reserves. He had already played over 50 league games.

WHAT DO WE SAY NOW? In 2003, Naylor's dream finally came true when Wolves reached the Premiership. A regular for some six seasons at Molineux, no-one deserved to taste the big time more than Lee – the club's longest-serving player along with goalkeeper Matt Murray.

LEON BRITTON

TOP TEEN RANKING IN 2000: 43 AGE NOW: 21

What's happened to him? West Ham paid Arsenal £400,000 for this teenage midfield prospect, but he joined Swansea without ever playing in The Hammers' first team.

LEON MIKE

TOP TEEN RANKING IN 2000: 44 AGE NOW: 22

What's happened to him? The England youth star bombed out at Man. City and joined Scottish outfit Aberdeen for a fee of £50,000 in the summer of 2002.

ANDY JOHNSON

TOP TEEN RANKING IN 2000: 45 AGE NOW: 22

What's happened to him? The livewire forward will feel he never really had a fair crack at Birmingham before his £750,000 switch to Crystal Palace in July 2002.

DAREL RUSSELL

TOP TEEN RANKING IN 2000: 47 AGE NOW: 22

What's happened to him? The midfielder usually has to make do with a place on the substitutes' bench at Norwich and may look elsewhere for regular first-team footy.

EZY IRIEKPEN

TOP TEEN RANKING IN 2000: 48 AGE NOW: 21

What's happened to him? The defender struggled to make it at West Ham – going out on loan spells to Leyton Orient and Cambridge United before being released.

ANTHONY GARDNER

TOP TEEN RANKING IN 2000: 50 AGE NOW: 22

WHAT DID WE SAY THEN? Back in early 2000, Gardner had just arrived at Spurs as part of their drive to snap up the country's top young players. He cost £1 million from Port Vale and the big 6ft 5in centre-back was set to improve greatly, learning from the likes of Sol Campbell.

WHAT DO WE SAY NOW? Gardner has yet to make 50 league appearances for Spurs and he has drifted in and out of Glenn Hoddle's team. In 2002-03 he missed several weeks with hamstring trouble and will be hoping he can now push Ledley King and Dean Richards for a place.

DELROY FACEY

TOP TEEN RANKING IN 2000: 49 AGE NOW: 23

What's happened to him? Some good displays for Huddersfield got the striker a big move to Bolton in 2002, where he's currently trying to win a first-team place.

SPELL CHECK STARS

Me flippin' computer's bust again – see if ya can work out who these geezers are! There's six points up for grabs!

1. Bar Ad Fiddle
2. Pale King Chess Key
3. Dairy Rice Vaseline

2 POINTS PER CORRECT ANSWER

Brazil lifted the World Cup in 2002.

second XI

Brazil are the best footy nation on Earth, but how much do ya know about dem silky Samba stars?

1 Edson Arantes do Nascimento is better known as which Brazilian footy legend?

2 In what year did Brazil win their first ever World Cup – was it 1938 or 1958?

3 Brazil won the 2002 World Cup, but which country did they beat in the final?

4 True or false? The real name of goofy Brazil star Ronaldinho is actually Ronaldo.

5 How many times have Brazil won the World Cup in their impressive history?

6 When was the last time Brazil got to host the finals of the World Cup?

7 Who did Brazil beat in the final of the 1994 World Cup, held in the USA, after a penalty shoot-out?

8 True or false? Rivaldo's footy mad girlfriend once held the world record for keepie-uppies.

9 Arsenal signed star midfielder Gilberto Silva from which club for £4.5 million?

10 Brazil play in their famous yellow shirts, but what is the colour of their current away shirt?

11 Ronaldinho hit the winner, but who scored Brazil's opening goal against England in their 2002 World Cup meeting?

1 POINT PER CORRECT ANSWER

TRANSFER TRACKER

Which wicked Euro star has played for these clubs during his career?

Willem II 1995-96

PSV 1996-1998

Man. United 1998-2001

Lazio 2001-2003

3 POINTS FOR CORRECT ANSWER

BALL GAMES

Now pay attention, coz this is tricky! Startin' at No.1, fill in da answers (the last letter of each answer is da first letter of the next), complete da circle and re-arrange the yellow letters to reveal a top Euro striker!

1. The club Zinedine Zidane left to join Real Madrid in 2001.
2. The nickname of Premiership club Southampton.
3. The first name of England Under-21 star Ameobi.
4. London club who won the FA Cup in 2003.
5. Tottenham Hotspur signed Robbie Keane from this club.
6. The surname of England winger 'Tricky Trev'.

10 POINTS FOR CORRECT ANSWER

LEGS ELEVEN

Which top young stars do these pins belong to?

2 POINTS PER CORRECT ANSWER (MAXIMUM 4)

anegrams

Rearrange these letters to find five wicked England stars – and grab yerself ten wicked points!

1. HI MEEKLY SEE
2. AT GREASE THOUGHT
3. CRASHES R MIND
4. FARM LAD PRANK
5. A NERVILY LEG

2 POINTS PER CORRECT ANSWER (MAXIMUM 10)

ALPHABET QUIZ

All the answers here begin with da letter 'T'!

1. Top Turkey midfielder who has played for Galatasaray, Rangers and Blackburn.
2. The nickname of Third Division Yorkshire outfit Huddersfield Town.
3. The surname of former Watford, Aston Villa and England gaffer, Graham.

2 POINTS PER CORRECT ANSWER (MAXIMUM 6)

SOL CAMPBELL QUIZ

Sol's a top player, but how much do ya know about da Arsenal man?

1 In what year was the big England defender born?

2 True or false? Sol's real name is actually Sulzeer.

3 Sol played his last game for Spurs in the FA Cup against which London club?

4 Campbell left Spurs for Arsenal in which year?

5 Against which country did Sol score his first international goal in 2002?

2 POINTS PER CORRECT ANSWER (MAXIMUM 10)

MATCH

Luis Figo ★ *Portugal*

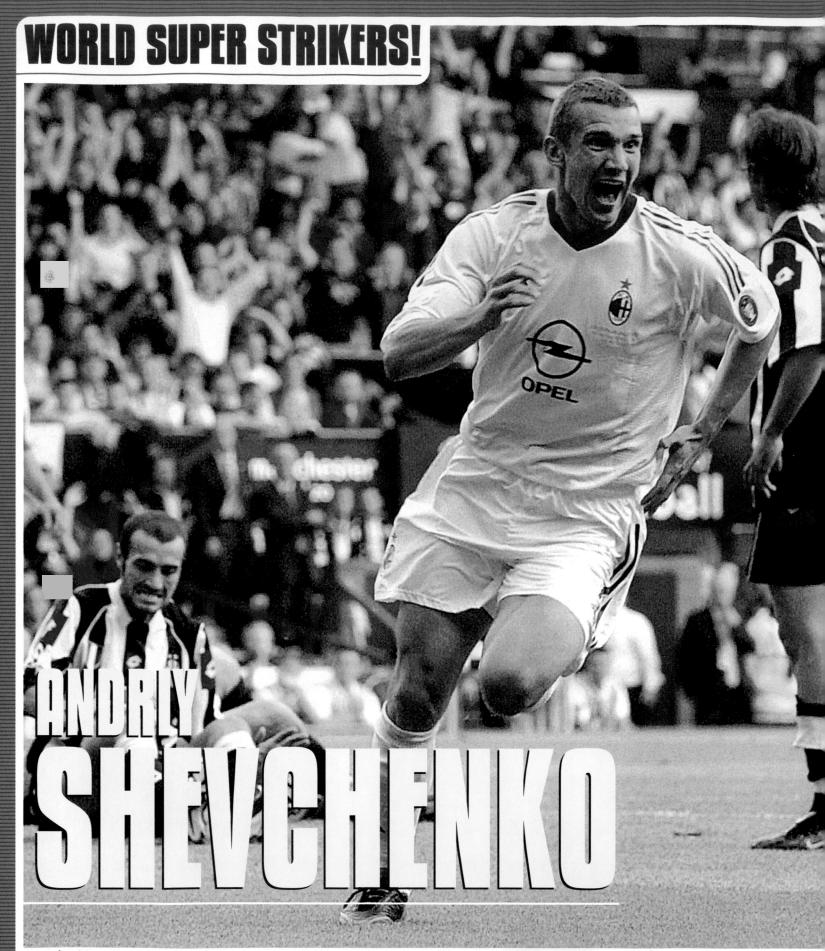

WORLD SUPER STRIKERS!

ANDRIY SHEVCHENKO

Andriy Shevchenko timeline...

October
DYNAMO DEBUT
Plays his first game for Kiev against Shakhtar Donetsk.

1994

November
EURO BOW
Makes his Champions League debut against Spartak Moscow.

December
OFF THE MARK
Scores his first Dynamo league goal in a 4-2 win over Dnipro.

1995

March
UKRAINE'S GAIN
Wins his first cap at international level as he plays for Ukraine against Croatia in a 4-0 win.

November
HAT-TRICK HERO
Blasts a fantastic hat-trick as Kiev sink Barcelona in the Nou Camp!

1997

April
TOP TON
Reaches a personal landmark with his 100th career goal for Dynamo against Zirka.

1999

July
MILAN MAGIC
Signs for Italian champions AC Milan in a £16 million deal.

August
DEBUT DELIGHT
Scores on his Milan debut as The Rossoneri draw 2-2 at Lecce.

November
EURO NO-GO
Ukraine lose to Slovenia in the Euro 2000 play-offs.

 46

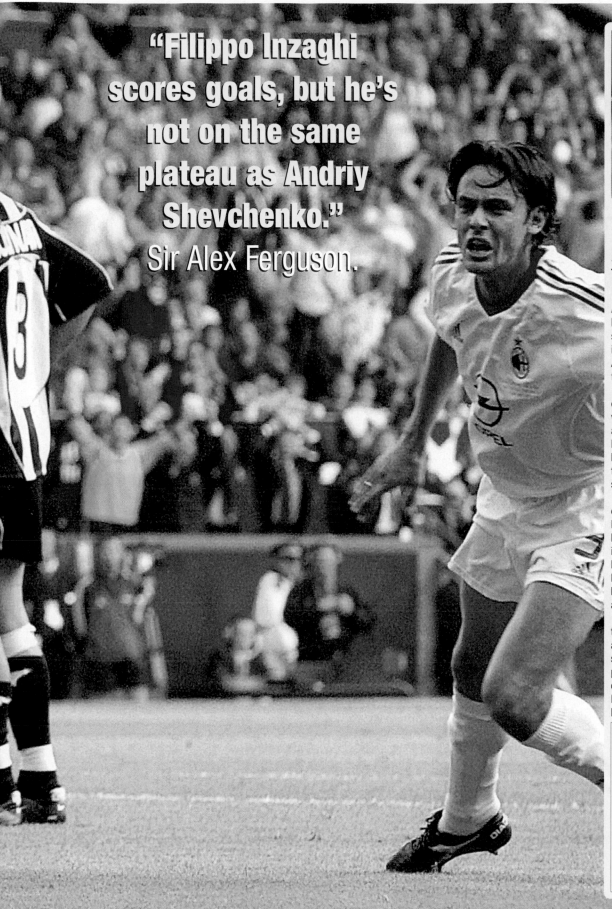

> ## "Filippo Inzaghi scores goals, but he's not on the same plateau as Andriy Shevchenko."
> Sir Alex Ferguson.

MATCH charts the rise of AC MILAN striker ANDRIY SHEVCHENKO!

Andriy Shevchenko made himself famous all over Europe in May 2003 when his ice-cool penalty in a tense shoot-out gave AC Milan victory in the Champions League final! And Sheva sunk Juventus to lift the famous trophy for the first time!

The Ukrainian has long been one of the world's top strikers, so it was no surprise that he ended up as Milan's match-winner. But while lifting the European Cup was the highlight of his career so far, he's fulfilled many of his ambitions since turning professional.

Born in a small village just outside the Ukrainian capital of Kiev, Shevchenko was snapped up by local side Dynamo and broke into the senior team at 17. It wasn't long before he was scoring goals left, right and centre for Kiev and he soon established a reputation as a striker with a golden future.

So how did Andriy make it to the top? And why is he still such a legend with the Kiev fans that shirts with his name on are more popular than some of Dynamo's current players? Read on, as MATCH reveals the highs and lows of Sheva's brilliant career!

CAREER FACTFILE

Born: September 29, 1976 in Kiev

Nationality: Ukrainian

Position: Striker

Height: 6ft

Weight: 11st 4lbs

Former clubs: Dynamo Kiev

Signed: From Dynamo Kiev for £16 million on July 2, 1999

Milan debut: v Lecce 29 August, 1999

Total Milan games/goals: 134/72 (August 1999 to May 2003)

International caps/goals: 48/21 (March 1995 to June 2003)

May

TOP GUN
Finishes as Serie A's top scorer in his first season with Milan, hitting 24 goals.

December

THIRD PLACE
Comes third in the European Footballer Of The Year awards.

2000

November

WORLD CUP WOE
Ukraine mess up their chance to reach the World Cup finals, losing a play-off to Germany.

2001

November

REAL ON THE RACK
Scores the only goal as Milan sink Real Madrid in the Champions League.

2002

November

SEMI STAR
Sends Milan to the Champions League final with a goal in the semi-final showdown with rivals Inter.

MATCH-WINNER
Sheva's penalty gives Milan the European Cup as Juve are beaten in the final.

May

2003

June

AT THE DOUBLE
Finishes the season in style with two goals for Ukraine in a 4-3 Euro 2004 qualifying win over Armenia.

1994

THE KIEV KID!

Andriy didn't waste much time bursting on to the professional scene in the Ukraine, because Dynamo Kiev couldn't wait to unleash him! Shevchenko was promoted to Kiev's senior squad at the age of 17 after top-scoring for their feeder team, Dynamo-2, in 1993-94. The following season, Sheva made his debut in the Ukraine league and was playing Champions League football within a month! Later that season in the same competition, he scored his first European goal, putting Kiev ahead in their home game against Bayern Munich.

1997

NOU CAMP HAT-TRICK!

In Sheva's first two seasons in Europe, Kiev had found it tough – they had defeated Panathinaikos 1-0 in 1995-96 but were banned for alleged bribery of a match official. And they had a nightmare in the following season, so 1997-98 required a big improvement and Dynamo, now inspired by Sheva, delivered. Linking up with strike partner Sergei Rebrov, Shevchenko was in devastating form. He scored in group matches against PSV and Newcastle before grabbing headlines all over Europe thanks to a sensational hat-trick against Barcelona in the Nou Camp! Barça had Rivaldo and Figo in their side but Shevchenko ran riot in Spain – scoring after ten and 33 minutes before sealing his treble with a penalty just before the break. Kiev finished top of the group but were beaten by eventual finalists Juventus in the quarter-finals. The deadly Sheva had already started to make a name for himself, though.

"I asked myself to kick the last penalty. I wasn't afraid, it was too important!"
— Andriy Shevchenko.

1998

DYNO-MITE KIEV!

The 1998-99 season was when Shevchenko and Dynamo Kiev were close to unstoppable. After reaching the Champions League quarter-finals the season before, the Ukrainian side were on a roll. Kiev were in a group with Lens and Arsenal but still finished top, with Andriy scoring in a 3-1 win over The Gunners. In the quarter-finals Kiev faced Real Madrid, but Sheva took charge, scoring three times over the two legs to put his side through. In the semis he put them ahead against Bayern, only for the Germans to claw it back to 3-3. A 1-0 defeat in the second leg stopped Kiev's Euro dream, but they won a domestic double in the Ukraine, and Sheva was the top scorer in the Champions League with ten goals.

1999

CIAO MILAN!

Europe's biggest clubs couldn't resist the bait any longer. After his stunning performances in Europe, Kiev resigned themselves to losing Shevchenko, and although Arsenal seemed interested in signing him as well as Dynamo team-mate Oleg Luzhny, it was AC Milan who nabbed him for £16 million. The Italian giants certainly had the pulling power. Milan had just won the Serie A title and the Italian's wealthy owner, Silvio Berlusconi, tempted Sheva with the promise of a huge salary – plus the use of his luxury yacht for a holiday, if he finished as the league's top scorer in his first season! So, after winning five league championships and three domestic cups for Kiev, Shevchenko joined Milan and began an exciting new chapter in his career as one of the hottest and most expensive strikers in the game.

1999

NOVEMBER SLOVENIA SHOCK!

In 1999, Ukraine were battling hard to qualify for a place at Euro 2000, and hopes were pinned on Sheva to guide them safely to the tournament. But they were trailing 1-0 to Russia in their final qualifying match until super Shevchenko popped up with a timely equaliser in the 87th minute to send Ukraine into a play-off match and send Russia out altogether! No-one fancied taking on Sheva's boys – and that included England manager Kevin Keegan, who was especially relieved to avoid them in the draw. So when Slovenia came out of the hat as their play-off opponents, the Ukrainians were red-hot favourites to qualify. Surprisingly, they lost the first leg 2-1 in Slovenia, but Andriy's 33rd-minute strike had given Ukraine a vital away goal to take home. In the second leg, Sergei Rebrov scored to draw level at 2-2 on aggregate – and qualifying for Holland and Belgium was within their reach. But a goal from Slovenia star Pavlin turned the tables upside down and sent the outsiders through. Sheva and his team-mates were left gutted.

2000

SERIE A SUPERSTAR!

Eager to make a good impression at AC Milan, Shevchenko got off to a flyer in Italy! He scored in his first ever game for The Rossoneri, a 2-2 draw at Lecce, and from then on he didn't look back. His best performances in his first season were a hat-trick against eventual title champs Lazio, a hat-trick against Perugia, both goals in Milan's 2-0 victory over rivals Juventus and the winner at Roma. Sheva also scored in both of the San Siro derbies against Inter – as Milan won one and lost one against their city rivals. But by the end of the league season, Milan had failed to retain the Serie A crown, finishing third behind Lazio and Juventus – while in Europe they crashed out of the Champions League at the first stage. But individually, Sheva was still covered in glory, as Italy's leading marksman with 24 league goals!

2001

JUNE SHEVCHENKO FOR SPURS?

Despite another successful season for Milan – after scoring another 24 goals and finishing as the second-top goalscorer in Italy – Sheva was linked with a move away from Serie A in 2001. Even stranger, he was tipped to join Spurs! The plan involved Shevchenko linking up with Ukrainian pal Sergei Rebrov, and rumours flew around that Tottenham were preparing a bid of £30 million! Speculation carried on for a few weeks until eventually Sheva announced his decision – he wanted to stay with Milan. And considering what happened to Rebrov at White Hart Lane, it was the right decision to make!

2001

NOVEMBER FALL GUYS AGAIN!

Two years on from flopping against Slovenia in the Euro 2000 play-offs, Ukraine were handed another chance to reach a major tournament. This time, after finishing second behind Poland in Group Five of their 2002 World Cup campaign, they faced Germany in a play-off decider. They looked confident and Sheva was in good form, scoring nine goals in qualifying. And Germany, after a 5-1 thrashing by England, were there for the taking. But it proved the same old story for the East Europeans. Shevchenko, who'd just recovered from plastic surgery to repair a broken nose, set up Ukraine's goal in Kiev as the first leg finished 1-1. And he struck again in the return leg in Dortmund, but it was only a consolation goal after Germany had scored four times! A 5-2 aggregate defeat meant Ukraine had failed again – a third play-off failure in a row.

2002

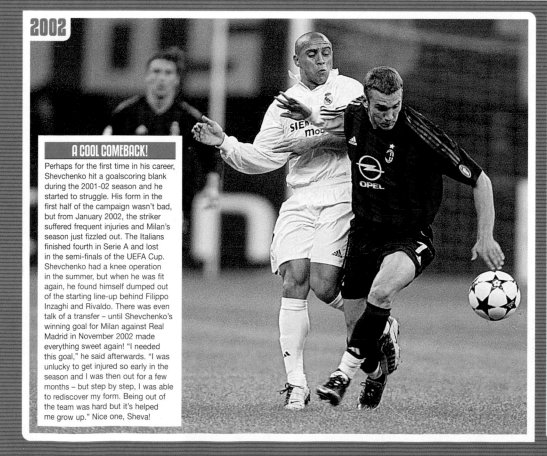

A COOL COMEBACK!

Perhaps for the first time in his career, Shevchenko hit a goalscoring blank during the 2001-02 season and he started to struggle. His form in the first half of the campaign wasn't bad, but from January 2002, the striker suffered frequent injuries and Milan's season just fizzled out. The Italians finished fourth in Serie A and lost in the semi-finals of the UEFA Cup. Shevchenko had a knee operation in the summer, but when he was fit again, he found himself dumped out of the starting line-up behind Filippo Inzaghi and Rivaldo. There was even talk of a transfer – until Shevchenko's winning goal for Milan against Real Madrid in November 2002 made everything sweet again! "I needed this goal," he said afterwards. "I was unlucky to get injured so early in the season and I was then out for a few months – but step by step, I was able to rediscover my form. Being out of the team was hard but it's helped me grow up." Nice one, Sheva!

2003

CHAMPIONS LEAGUE HERO!

Boosted by that goal against Real, Sheva's confidence returned. Milan, after challenging hard for the Serie A championship for most of the season, dropped out of the domestic title race but continued to progress in the Champions League. In the semi-finals against Inter Milan, the Ukrainian scored a crucial goal in the second leg which took his team through to the final on the away goals rule. The final itself was an all-Italian affair, with Milan facing Serie A champions Juventus. As expected, it was a tight affair with defences on top. Sheva scored in the first half, only to have it ruled out for offside, but he wasn't to be denied. When a marathon match eventually went to penalties, Andriy took the crucial spot-kick. And he showed no sign of nerves as he stepped up and blasted it past Gianluigi Buffon to make Milan European champions! "It was the most important goal of my career – it's a dream come true," revealed an emotional Andriy after the highlight of his career so far.

FREDDY ADU!

MEET THE MEGASTAR OF TOMORROW!

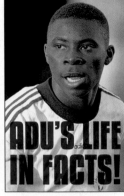

ADU'S LIFE IN FACTS!

1 Super striker Freddy Adu was born in Ghana and grew up playing footy in his bare feet. He didn't wear his first pair of boots until he was eight!

2 When he was eight years old, Adu's mum Emelia won a green card lottery – where foreigners can win the chance to live in the USA. This is how he came to live and play in the United States!

3 In the first hole of golf Adu ever played – a 370-yard par-four – he hit the green in two, before two-putting for par! It's now his second favourite sport!

4 When he was ten, Freddy travelled to Italy with a US team for an Under-14 tournament against Lazio and Juventus. Freddy's team won the competition, he was the top scorer and was voted Most Valuable Player.

5 In his first ever organised basketball game at the age of 11, Adu scored a wicked 28 points!

6 As an 11-year-old, in the first county art competition he entered, Adu won the first prize!

7 In 35 US Under-17 matches in 2002, Freddy scored 22 goals – and he was only 12!

8 On February 12, 2002, he notched both goals for his US Under-17 team in a 2-1 exhibition victory over Chicago Fire – the USA league winners!

9 Freddy's fave film is the 2001 smash hit 'Fellowship Of The Ring'!

10 In the latest 'Championship Manager' game, Freddy is earmarked as a top up-and-coming star!

He might only be 14, but USA goal ace Freddy Adu is already being hailed as the next footy superstar!

There's a wicked new sheriff in town in America – and his name is Freddy Adu! The young striker is being tipped as the new Pele, after scoring 22 goals in 35 matches for the US under-17s team last year – when he was still only 12 years old!

Now 14, he's got a Nike deal worth £1 million, and Inter Milan tried to sign him for £5 million! Adu's not in a hurry to move, but he's still got loads of ambitions! **"I see myself in a World Cup final for the USA,"** says Freddy.

"We'll be playing against a top team that everyone picks to win. One day when I'm holding that World Cup trophy, someone's gonna take a picture."

Now don't go forgetting where you first heard the name of super Freddy Adu – MATCH of course!

FREDDY ADU FACTFILE

Club: Potomac Cougars
Born: June 2, 1989 in Ghana
Height: 5ft 8ins
Weight: 64kg
Nationality: American
Position: Striker

MATCH

WORLD SUPERSTARS

Zinedine Zidane ★ France

WHO THE STAR

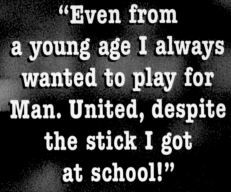

The top stars might love the clubs they play for now, but it doesn't necessarily mean they followed

DAVID BECKHAM

> Currently plays for: **Real Madrid**
> Supported as a kid: **Man. United**

My dad loved football and had always supported Man. United. I always wanted to be a footballer, and even from a young age I wanted to play for Man. United, despite the stick I got at school! So when I finally signed for United – the team I'd supported and the team my dad had supported all his life – it was one of the proudest days of my life. It was a dream come true for the whole family.

CARLTON COLE

> Currently plays for: **Chelsea**
> Supported as a kid: **Chelsea**

I always supported Chelsea, because even though my local club was Brentford, the biggest team that were close to me was Chelsea. I supported them from about the age of 12 or 13, because my uncle used to talk about them all the time.

ROBBIE KEANE

> Currently plays for: **Tottenham Hotspur**
> Supported as a kid: **Liverpool**

I was a Liverpool fan when I was younger and Ian Rush was my hero. In those days he was a top name and used to score every week, so I wanted to be like him! He's been a big influence, because I used to watch him and tried to copy him. He was a great player for a long time. All my family were Liverpool fans so I had no choice – I had to follow them!

SHOLA AMEOBI

> Currently plays for: **Newcastle United**
> Supported as a kid: **Newcastle United**

The black and white is drummed into you – that's how I became a fan. I'd always wanted to play for the club, as I'm sure most boys in Newcastle want to today. It's part and parcel of growing up in a city where your mums – and particularly your dads – want you to watch and play for the team. As a Newcastle fan I looked up to players in the past and now I'm playing, I know what it must have been like for them.

GARETH SOUTHGATE

> Currently plays for: **Middlesbrough**
> Supported as a kid: **Man. United**

I was always a Man. United fan, because Bryan Robson was my favourite player when I was young. I was lucky enough to work with Bryan when I played for England a few years ago – and he was a coach when Terry Venables was in charge of the national side. That was a brilliant experience for me.

> "Even from a young age I always wanted to play for Man. United, despite the stick I got at school!"
>
> David Beckham

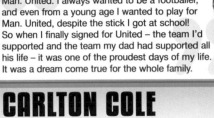

S SUPPORTED!

them when they were little 'uns! **MATCH** *digs deep to find out who the stars supported as youngsters!*

ALAN SMITH

> Currently plays for: **Leeds United**
> Supported as a kid: **Leeds United**

I've been at Leeds United since I was ten years old and obviously it's my home-town club, so this has become like a second home to me really. To be honest, the club has always been a massive part of my life. It's been good to me for a long time and hopefully that will continue in the future.

GARETH BARRY

> Currently plays for: **Aston Villa**
> Supported as a kid: **Tottenham Hotspur**

I supported Tottenham when I was younger. I enjoyed the way they played and the club had some great players back in those days as well. Paul Gascoigne was definitely my favourite player. I remember when he scored that free-kick in the FA Cup semi-final against Arsenal in 1991 when we beat them 3-2. I think that's probably the best Spurs game I've ever seen!

DANNY MURPHY

> Currently plays for: **Liverpool**
> Supported as a kid: **Liverpool**

Liverpool were the club I'd always supported. Thousands of kids would love to play for their favourite team, and that's all I wanted to do. I used to watch the games at Anfield, and luckily I caught Kenny Dalglish's last couple of years – he was my hero. Then it was John Barnes as I got older and I've been fortunate enough to meet them both since, so I'm very lucky!

MICHAEL TONGE

> Currently plays for: **Sheffield United**
> Supported as a kid: **Man. City**

I didn't actually support Sheffield United when I was younger. I'm from Manchester, so I was always a Man. City supporter back then. It's pretty funny though, because I always used to notice Sheffield United's results. But I didn't support them until I started playing for the club!

PAUL SCHOLES

> Currently plays for: **Man. United**
> Supported as a kid: **Man. United**

I supported Manchester United when I was young, but my dad was an Oldham fan so I got used to watching them when they were in cup finals and getting promoted. But yes, I was always a United fan. It's like living a dream really, being a local lad and joining the club from school. Sometimes you don't realise how lucky you are to be playing for one of the best teams in the world.

Sven took charge of England in 2001.

third XI

Every team's gotta 'ave a gaffer, but how much do ya really know about da big-time bosses?

1 Who was in charge of England when they won the World Cup final at Wembley back in 1966?

2 True or false? Gerard Houllier worked as a teacher in Liverpool before managing the club.

3 Before Sir Bobby Robson took over, who was the manager of Newcastle United?

4 Portsmouth boss Harry Redknapp has a famous footy star son – but what's the name of his lad?

5 True or false? Man. United gaffer Sir Alex Ferguson has managed Scotland.

6 In which year did Arsene Wenger take over at Arsenal – 1994, 1995 or 1996?

7 Who was in charge of West Ham on the day they were relegated in 2003?

8 Which famous old Nationwide club did ace Scottish boss David Moyes manage before Everton?

9 Sven Goran Eriksson is the England gaffer, but who is his assistant?

10 True or false? George Graham has managed both Spurs and Arsenal.

11 How many Premiership championships has Kenny Dalglish won in his time as a manager?

1 POINT PER CORRECT ANSWER

Those Were The Days

Liverpool won the FA Cup in 2001, but who scored da winnin' goal against Arsenal?

THE F.A. CUP SPONSORED BY AXA
WINNERS 2001

THE F.A. CUP SPONSORED BY AXA
WINNERS 2001

3 POINTS FOR CORRECT ANSWER

WHO IS MR POTATO?

Can ya figure out which of me footy mates 'as been dressed up like a big, bad potato?

4 POINTS FOR CORRECT ANSWER

JUAN VERON QUIZ

He may be an Argie, but this baldy star has got a few tricks up his sleeve! How much do ya know about 'im?

1 Man. United paid how much for Seba when he signed from Lazio in 2001?

2 Veron scored his first competitive goal for United against which club?

3 Juan's nickname in Argentina is 'Brujita', but what does it mean?

4 True or false? Veron's dad used to play for Argie club Estudiantes.

5 Veron has been around for a long time now, but exactly how old is he?

2 POINTS PER CORRECT ANSWER (MAXIMUM 10)

player match-up

Try an' work out where these top footy stars were born! There's a massive 12 points if ya can!

1. Ryan Giggs	A. Liverpool
2. Wayne Rooney	B. Marseille
3. Kieron Dyer	C. Cardiff
4. Danny Murphy	D. Romford
5. Zinedine Zidane	E. Ipswich
6. Ray Parlour	F. Chester

2 POINTS PER CORRECT ANSWER (MAXIMUM 12)

KIT KINGS

Which Premiership team used to wear this mingin' kit a few years back?

2 POINTS FOR CORRECT ANSWER

Who Am I?

Read all da clues and look at the pics to try an' figure out which top footy star this is!

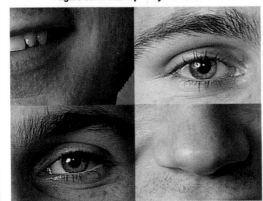

1. I was born in 1978 in Romford.
2. I joined West Ham and played over 130 games.
3. In 1995 I went on loan to Swansea City.
4. I was signed by Chelsea for £11 million in 2001.
5. I play in centre midfield.

5 POINTS FOR CORRECT ANSWER

TABLE TOPPERS

In wot year did the Prem finish up like this?

1.	Man. United	84
2.	Aston Villa	74
3.	Norwich City	72
16.	Crystal Palace	49
17.	Middlesbrough	44
18.	Nottingham Forest	40

2 POINTS FOR CORRECT ANSWER

DREAM TEAM

Use da clues to discover this awesome footy team of top stars! See how many points ya can get here!

GK Germany's ogre-like shot-stopper who was brilliant at the 2002 World Cup.

RB Energetic Brazil and AC Milan right-back who could run all day long.

CB Manchester United ace who was signed from Leeds for £30 million in 2002.

CB Classy Italy international who moved from Lazio to AC Milan in 2002.

LB Liverpool's muscular Norway international who's got a rock-hard six-pack.

RM Tricky Portuguese winger who has played for both Barcelona and Real Madrid in Spain.

CM Curly-haired Wales international at Spurs.

CM Germany international who left Bayer Leverkusen for Bayern Munich in 2002.

LM Juventus and Czech star with blonde hair.

ST Geordie hitman who used to captain England.

ST Powerful Inter Milan and Italy striker who scores goals for fun.

1 POINT PER CORRECT ANSWER (MAXIMUM 11)

WORLD SUPERSTARS

Ronaldinho ★ *Brazil*

SHEARER: MY

Alan Shearer will go down as one of the most prolific goalscorers in the history of English football. Since making a sensational goalscoring debut for Southampton back in 1988, Shearer has been one of the most talked-about and popular footballers in the country – banging in hundreds of goals for Blackburn Rovers, Newcastle United and England.

His traditional celebration salute has been seen over 300 times in all competitions and he's broken record upon record. He's been the most expensive player in the world, the top scorer in an international tournament and the man who sunk Germany at Euro 2000 to give England their first victory over their fierce rivals for 34 years!

He's been named Player Of The Year twice, won the Premiership title, turned down a move to Man. United and battled back from career-threatening injuries. He's also a hero with the Newcastle fans – who are praying he carries on playing for as long as possible – and he's been missed by England since his international retirement.

But Alan Shearer isn't finished yet. The super striker remains a key part of Bobby Robson's Newcastle team and would love to win something for The Magpies before he calls it a day. Now it's time for MATCH to pay tribute to one of the best strikers of the last 20 years, so get ready for the best moments of his amazing career so far!

▲ HAT-TRICK HERO FOR SOUTHAMPTON!

If Alan Shearer was an unknown when he made his full debut for Southampton on April 9, 1988, the 'nobody' tag didn't last very long – it was only a few minutes into the game against Arsenal at The Dell when he scored his first Saints goal! By the end of the match, the 17-year-old striker had incredibly helped himself to a hat-trick! But there was still one problem. **"I hadn't thought about how to celebrate in front of so many people,"** said Al. **"So I just ran around for a while flapping my arms about and savouring the moment!"**

SCRAPBOOK!

◄ ENGLAND CALLING!

After doing well for the England Under-21 side, Alan made his full debut against France in February 1992. And surprise, surprise, he scored! Shearer got the first then set up Gary Lineker for the second.

▲ PREMIERSHIP WIN!

The 1994-95 season was one of the best of Alan Shearer's career so far. He slammed in 34 league goals, won the Golden Boot award for being the league's highest scorer, was voted PFA Player Of The Year, and helped Rovers to win the Premiership title! Blackburn took the crown by a single point from Man. United when results went their way on the final day of a dramatic season. **"It was the first honour I'd won as part of a team, and what a team it was!"** said a delighted Shearer. **"We weren't just successful, but entertaining too."**

◄ SHEARER THE ROVER!

Southampton couldn't hold on to their star striker forever, and in the summer of 1992 Blackburn pounced with a hefty bid for the 22-year-old. Rovers had just been promoted to the newly-formed Premiership and they meant business. The Lancashire club offered a British record fee of £3.3 million for Big Al, who couldn't refuse! **"Signing for Blackburn was one of the best things I ever did in my life,"** he said. **"I joined them because I knew it would be a good career move."** Boss Kenny Dalglish built a winning team around Shearer.

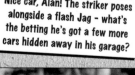

Nice car, Alan! The striker poses alongside a flash Jag - what's the betting he's got a few more cars hidden away in his garage?

◄ EURO HERO! ►

It was the summer of 1996 and the whole country had gone footy crazy! When the European Championships were staged in England, everyone got behind Terry Venables's side, and the team starred Alan Shearer as the centre-forward. Despite a bad run of form for his country going into the tournament, Al kept his place in the side and repaid his coach's faith by scoring five goals to become the top goalscorer. But Euro '96 ended on a sour note for the England team when they lost out on penalties to rivals Germany in the semi-finals. **"My biggest disappointment was not winning Euro '96,"** Shearer told MATCH years later. **"We'll never have a better chance of winning a major tournament, but we gave it our very best shot and we only went out on penalties in the end."**

SHEARER'S big moments!

APRIL 1988

Alan Shearer made his full debut for Southampton against Arsenal at The Dell aged just 17 years and 240 days. It was a sensational performance as he scored a hat-trick, and a week later The Saints gave him a pro contract. In his first year, Al was on £225 a week!

JUNE 1991

Very early on in his career, Shearer faced one of the biggest matches of his entire life – he got married! He and Lainya tied the knot at St James' Church in Southampton after Al had returned from England Under-21 duty in the Toulon tournament. He had been an outstanding success for his country. England won the competition and Shearer was the top scorer with seven goals. He was also named as the Player Of The Tournament.

AUGUST 1991

The new Southampton star found it hard to get a goalscoring run going for the first two seasons, but Shearer started the 1991-92 campaign playing under a new coach – Ian Branfoot. He thrived with Branfoot, scoring 13 goals in Division One and 21 in all competitions, to top the club's scoring charts and establish a reputation as one of England's top young strikers.

FEBRUARY 1992

Shearer's form impressed England manager Graham Taylor, who called him into the full national squad for a friendly against France at Wembley. And just like his Southampton debut, Shearer delivered on the big stage, scoring in a 2-0 victory. His name was in the headlines and up in lights!

JUNE 1992

The talented young striker made it into England's squad for the summer's European Championships in Sweden but had a quiet tournament as the whole team struggled badly. England failed to win any of their three group matches against Sweden, Denmark and France, and crashed out before the knockout stages. Shearer made one appearance, playing 90 minutes in the 0-0 draw with France.

JULY 1992

Ambitious Blackburn Rovers, newly promoted to the top flight under boss Kenny Dalglish, moved for Shearer. Man. United were also keen to sign him, but Rovers got their man for a British record fee of £3.3 million and Shearer's Saints days were over.

AUGUST 1992

The man with the uncanny knack of scoring on his debut was at it again for Rovers. This time, Shearer scored twice in a thrilling 3-3 draw against Crystal Palace, and both goals were crackers from outside the box! He settled into life at Blackburn with ease and just couldn't stop scoring.

DECEMBER 1992

After a fantastic first half of his first season with Blackburn, Al's season faltered. He scored two goals against Leeds on Boxing Day but then went off with a knee injury. He had an operation to remove damaged cartilage but found he'd snapped his cruciate knee ligament. His season was over and Blackburn finished fourth.

After his superb displays at Euro '96, Shearer became a man in demand, with some of the biggest clubs in Europe after his signature! Everton, Liverpool, Arsenal, Man. United, Barcelona, Inter Milan and Juventus were all keen to secure his services, but after several days of agonising over his next move, Shearer plumped for Kevin Keegan's Newcastle! He joined his boyhood favourites for a staggering £15.6 million fee – which at the time was a world record – and was welcomed to St James' Park by 15,000 Shearer-mad Geordies! **"I'm not normally an emotional person, but when I was paraded before the Newcastle fans, the sight of 15,000 supporters waiting in the rain to greet me brought a lump to my throat,"** said a touched Shearer. He would soon repay their faith.

▲ COME IN NO.9!

Alan was desperate to follow in the footsteps of his Newcastle heroes by claiming the famous No.9 shirt, the traditional number held by all centre-forwards. It was already taken by his England pal Les Ferdinand – but Les agreed to surrender the number to his new £15 million team-mate and the duo formed a fine partnership up front for The Magpies. Between them, Al and Les hit 49 goals in 1996-97.

▲ ENGLAND'S PROUD LEADER!

With Terry Venables stepping down as the England coach after Euro '96, a new manager was needed. Glenn Hoddle took over and immediately chose Alan as his captain. Shearer's first match as skipper was against Moldova in September 1996, but it was the home game against Poland in October which left a lasting impression on the Newcastle striker. **"I always dreamed of playing for England but never dreamed of captaining them. My first game as England captain at Wembley was the best moment of my international career. Leading the team out to play against Poland in front of 80,000 fans while wearing the armband made me so proud."** For good measure, Al scored both goals in a 2-1 win!

Shearer practises his ball skills at St James' Park. Can you possibly guess who sponsored Newcastle United during that season?

◀ MAULING UNITED!

When Manchester United came to Newcastle in October 1996, Shearer and his team-mates had revenge in mind. Back in August of that year, United had ruined Shearer's big Toon debut in the Charity Shield, cruising to a 4-0 win. But it was a different story at St James' Park as The Magpies ran out 5-0 winners – dishing out United's worst league defeat for 12 years in the process! Shearer got one of the goals, along with Ferdinand, Albert, Ginola and Peacock! **"I had been taunted by them all throughout the game, so it was nice to celebrate right under their noses,"** he remembered.

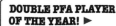

DOUBLE PFA PLAYER OF THE YEAR! ▶

To be named PFA Player Of The Year is a great achievement, but to win it twice is extra special! Shearer's first success came in 1995 when Rovers won the Premiership title. His next success in winning the award – voted by his fellow players – was after his first season at Newcastle in 1997.

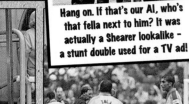

SHEAR AGONY! ▶

After his successful first season at Newcastle, Shearer couldn't wait for his second – but it didn't even start as disaster struck in a pre-season game. **"I stretched to knock the ball through to a team-mate and it skidded away from me on the wet surface,"** said Alan. **"My studs got caught in the turf and my body weight was thrown forward. There was a loud crack and I knew right away that something serious had happened."** Shearer had fractured a fibula, ruptured ligaments in his ankle and chipped a bone too.

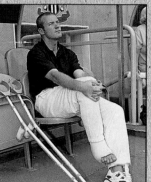

Hang on. If that's our Al, who's that fella next to him? It was actually a Shearer lookalike – a stunt double used for a TV ad!

Shearer spent months out injured and working his way back to full fitness, and it was a frustrating time for both him and Newcastle – who obviously missed him. But their star striker was back in action in January 1998 against unlikely opponents – Stevenage Borough. Shearer scored in the FA Cup fourth round game at Stevenage, earning a 1-1 draw, then claimed both goals in the replay at St James' Park. Shearer was back!

◀ COMEBACK BEGINS!

◀ SEMI GLORY... ▶

When Newcastle reached the FA Cup semi-finals in 1998 and 1999, it was Shearer who helped steer them into the final. In 1998, Al hit the winner over Sheffield United. And a year later, Shearer scored twice in extra-time against Spurs to send The Toon Army through to Wembley. But if he had the magic touch in semi-finals...

Alan remembered his days as a fan in 2000 when he launched the MATCH and Nationwide Fan Of The Year award!

◀ ... BUT CUP FINAL WOE!

...it deserted him in the finals. On both occasions, Shearer was unable to inspire his team to glory. In 1998 Newcastle lost 2-0 to Arsenal, and a year later, the Toon were outclassed by Man. United 2-0. Then in 2000, Newcastle blew a chance to make it third time lucky, as they lost in the semis to eventual winners Chelsea!

SHEARER'S big moments!

MAY 1994
Fully fit again, Shearer had a cracking 1993-94 season. He scored a wicked 31 league goals – Blackburn's next highest scorer was Kevin Gallacher on seven – as Rovers finished runners-up in the Premier League. As an added bonus, Shearer was also voted the Football Writers' Player Of The Year!

MARCH 1995
Rovers and Shearer were determined to go one better and land the league title in 1994-95 and they were in the hunt all season. Shearer, of course, was in tremendous form as usual and passed an important landmark during the course of the season. In March 1995 he scored the 100th goal of his career in a game against Chelsea.

MAY 1995
The title run-in was nail-biting, but Rovers hung on to a lead to take it from Man. United by a single point. Going into the final match, either side could have won. Blackburn lost at Liverpool, but it didn't matter because United only drew at West Ham. Rovers won the championship and Shearer was named PFA Player Of The Year for his 34-goal return that season.

JUNE 1996
Despite a lengthy run of international games without a goal – his last had been against the USA back in 1994 – Shearer was still England's first-choice striker for the 1996 European Championships. It was a good decision by coach Terry Venables, as Shearer scored five goals to finish as the competition's leading marksman as England reached the semi-finals.

JULY 1996
After his performances at Euro '96, Shearer was in demand from clubs at home and across Europe. Man. United looked like the hot favourites to clinch his signature in the summer of 1996, but the lure of joining his home-town club was too much and the forward signed for Newcastle. The transfer fee was a world record £15.6 million!

AUGUST 1996
For once, a Shearer debut didn't go to plan, as The Magpies were beaten 4-0 by Man. United in the Charity Shield, then lost their first game of the season at Everton. But things picked up and Shearer was soon a regular scorer. His first goal for Newcastle came in his home debut against Wimbledon, and he ended the season with 25 goals to finish the club's top scorer.

SEPTEMBER 1996
England started the qualifying games for the 1998 World Cup with Glenn Hoddle as their new coach, and he selected a new national team captain – Alan Shearer! Shearer's first match as skipper came in the 3-0 victory in Moldova, and he scored in that too!

JUNE 1997
There was no chance of a rest for Al, even though he'd had to undergo groin operations during a busy first season with Newcastle. In June he starred in Le Tournoi, a tournament involving England, France, Brazil and Italy, and supposedly a good warm-up for the following year's World Cup. England won it and Shearer scored the only goal in the France game.

JULY 1997
Disaster struck as Alan prepared for the 1997-98 season under new Newcastle manager Kenny Dalglish. Playing in the pre-season Umbro Tournament, he broke his leg and injured ankle ligaments. A long time on the sidelines looked on the cards.

JANUARY 1998
The long road back to fitness started with Big Al finally making his return against Bolton in a 2-1 win. Progress was slow, but the striker still scored a couple of league goals before the end of the season, and was on the scoresheet during Newcastle's run to the FA Cup final. Sadly, there was no fairytale ending as The Magpies lost 2-0 to Arsenal at Wembley.

England's skipper was busy in the run-up to Euro 2000 - but he still found time to sign some shirts for his fave footy mag!

ARGY-BARGY AT THE WORLD CUP! ▶

Shearer missed out on the 1994 World Cup finals after England failed to qualify, but he was the proud captain of his country when the team took part in the world's biggest tournament four years later in France. Hopes of doing well in the competition were high – especially after Shearer put England ahead in the first group game against Tunisia. Glenn Hoddle's side made the second round after beating the Tunisians 2-0 and Colombia by the same scoreline. England then faced old rivals Argentina. Shearer did his bit, scoring during the 2-2 draw in normal time, but The Three Lions lost after a dramatic penalty shoot-out and went home early.

SHEARER BENCHED? ▶

Alan Shearer undroppable? Not in Ruud Gullit's eyes! After a bad start to the 1999-2000 season, the heat was on Newcastle's coach and he resorted to drastic action for the clash with derby rivals Sunderland – Shearer was dropped! The decision backfired on Gullit – Newcastle lost 2-1 and the coach quit days later. When new boss Bobby Robson was brought in, it signalled the beginning of a revival. **"To find myself on the bench was a big shock,"** said Al. **"Ruud told me I wasn't worthy of a place in the side. I didn't agree."**

Shearer and England pal Michael Owen posed as fighter pilots in 2000 as they launched their new MACH Speed boots!

▲ GIMME THAT BALL!

Luxembourg were always on a hiding to nothing when they faced England at Wembley in September 1999. The Three Lions were chasing Euro 2000 qualification and little Luxembourg were no match for Kevin Keegan's team. Shearer led the way as usual with an impressive hat-trick and he claimed the matchball afterwards!

◀ FIVE GOAL SPREE!

As if to prove a massive point to his former boss Gullit, Shearer showed straight away that the Dutchman had been wrong to drop him for the match against Sunderland. Back in the team under Bobby Robson, he helped himself to an amazing five goals as Newcastle romped to an 8-0 win over Sheffield Wednesday!

GERMANY GROUNDED! ▶

England hadn't beaten a Germany side since the World Cup in 1966, but that miserable run ended in this Euro 2000 game – thanks to Shearer! Al's header won the game and he said afterwards: **"You could see the elation on my face when I scored but it was nothing compared to what I felt at the final whistle!"** Shearer also scored during the next game against Romania, but England lost the game 3-2 and went out of the competition. That proved to be Shearer's last game in an England shirt after 63 caps and 30 goals.

▲ A DAY AT THE OFFICE!

"So I cut the ribbon and run round with a trolley, right?" Shearer opens Umbro's new headquarters in 2000!

▲ ROY RAGE!

Shearer has had some fierce clashes in his career, but none more so than in September 2001. Newcastle beat Man. United 4-3 and Al scored the late winner. But Roy Keane lost his rag with the Newcastle skipper in injury time and tried to punch him in the face! Keane was sent off and Shearer celebrated a great win.

SPOT THE DIFFERENCE!

HELP MAKE A DIFFERENCE

BACK TO BASICS! ▶

Big Al has never forgotten his roots, and in 2002 he jumped at the chance to re-visit his childhood footy team, Wallsend Boys' Club. Waiting for him there was a special poster showing him first as a young lad, and then in his current status as Newcastle's captain! **"I always wanted to play for Newcastle,"** Alan told MATCH.

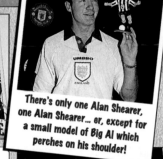

There's only one Alan Shearer, one Alan Shearer... or, except for a small model of Big Al which perches on his shoulder!

IT'S 300 UP FOR THE SUPER STRIKER! ▲

On October 19, 2002, Shearer reached a fantastic milestone. He scored the 300th goal of his legendary career – against former club Blackburn! Of course, MATCH was on hand with an exclusive interview to mark the special occasion, and Alan couldn't hide his delight. He had already bagged the Premiership record of 200 goals just a few months earlier. **"I suppose records are there to be broken by someone, someday,"** he said. **"I'm not sure how long it will last, but I'm very proud that I've done it and I realise how lucky I am to be in this great game."** No matter how many more goals he scores by the time he retires from football, Alan Shearer will always be remembered as one of England's finest strikers!

"Aye, but do you think it's clear that this book is about me?"

SHEARER'S big moments!

MAY 1998
At last Al had returned to something approaching his best form, and he travelled to France for the World Cup as England's main striker and skipper. He scored England's first goal of the tournament in the 2-0 victory over Tunisia and against Argentina in the second round. But England lost that match in a penalty shoot-out – even though Shearer scored his spot-kick.

MAY 1999
Newcastle's 1998-99 season started in turmoil, with Kenny Dalglish replaced by Ruud Gullit in a bid to make the team play more attractive football. Newcastle didn't do much better but reached a second successive FA Cup final and Shearer scored 14 league goals. But Newcastle lost another final, beaten 2-0 by Man. United.

AUGUST 1999
Shearer suffered a tough start to the 1999-2000 season. First he was sent off against Aston Villa on the opening day of the new campaign – which also happened to be his 100th appearance for Newcastle. And later that month he was left on the bench for the derby against Sunderland as Gullit wanted to prove a point. But just two days later, Gullit resigned.

SEPTEMBER 1999
A change in fortune happened almost immediately for Shearer. At club level, Bobby Robson was named as the new Newcastle manager, which seemed to please everyone – including the club's star striker. As if to emphasise this, he scored five goals in an 8-0 romp against Sheffield Wednesday! Then in a Euro 2000 qualifier against lowly Luxembourg, Alan scored his first ever England hat-trick in a 6-0 rout.

JUNE 2000
Having scored 25 league goals, his best tally for three seasons, Shearer must have been in confident mood as he captained England in the 2000 European Championships. But he had already announced his intention to retire from international football after the championships, and The Three Lions flopped in the tournament. He bowed out in some style though, scoring England's winner against rivals Germany in the group stages.

DECEMBER 2000
Free from the pressures of captaining his country, Al was able to concentrate completely on Newcastle. But things didn't go according to plan – an old injury refused to go away and he had to undergo surgery to cure tendonitis in his knee. As a result, he missed out on the rest of the 2000-01 season.

APRIL 2002
Shearer reached an impressive footy landmark when he scored his 200th Premiership goal on April 20th, 2002. The Newcastle ace grabbed his team's third in a 3-0 victory over Charlton, leaving his nearest challenger in the goalscoring stakes – Andy Cole – well behind on 139 Premiership strikes.

MAY 2002
Back to his best, Shearer finished the 2001-02 term as one of the sharpest strikers in the Premiership. His final tally of 23 league goals placed him just one behind the overall leading goalscorer, Thierry Henry, and level with both Ruud van Nistelrooy and Jimmy Floyd Hasselbaink.

FEBRUARY 2003
Shearer scored the 15th hat-trick of his glorious career in a big game for Newcastle, notching a terrific treble in the Champions League match against German side Bayer Leverkusen.

APRIL 2003
Alan was honoured with a deserved prize at the PFA awards in London. As well as being named in the PFA Premiership Team Of The Season, Shearer was also announced as the Premier League's Overall Player Of The Decade. Earlier in the month, he had been named Domestic Player Of The Decade. You deserve it Big Al!

>FOOTY MAD!<

CAPTION CRAZY!

MATCH loves having a laugh at the world of footy -
take a look at some of this year's wicked pictures!

Charlton discovered who had been putting itching powder in their shorts!

Graham Taylor puts his finger on Aston Villa's problem.

Birds just love the West Brom players!

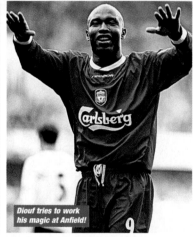

Diouf tries to work his magic at Anfield!

After he piled on the pounds, Man. United couldn't wait to get rid of David Beckham!

Gary Neville didn't think much to England's pre-match meal.

When David Moyes told Wayne Rooney to lie low for a bit, he didn't quite have this in mind.

MATCH

WORLD SUPERSTARS

Michael Owen ★ England

SEAMO ON

*Ever wondered what it's like to play in a dramatic penalty shoot-out? **MATCH** asked **MANCHESTER***

⭐ **So why are you so good at saving penalties, Seamo? Do you have any secret tactics you can tell us?**
"I just look at the run-up of whoever's taking the penalty! The way they approach the ball dictates which way I go. If the striker does something you're not expecting – like Dwight Yorke did against me once when he just chipped it down the centre of the goal – then they'll probably score."

⭐ **So it surprised you when Yorkie did that from the spot against you?**
"Well it was a fantastic piece of skill, but the next time I faced Dwight he pulled it wide. He would have scored that time too, because I just stood still after what he'd

done before! That's all it is, though. You look at the run-up and make your decision quickly."

⭐ **So you judge each run-up – you don't remember which way strikers go?**
"Sometimes people say, 'He'll hit it this way' or 'He always puts it that way,' but if you look at a good penalty taker, he'll always vary the way he takes it and which side of the goal he puts the ball."

⭐ **Did Bob Wilson, your old coach at Arsenal, make you study the run-up?**
"No, he always told me to stand still and move after the ball had been hit, so we actually had a difference of opinion. That's what Shilts – Peter Shilton – tried

to do for England in the 1990 World Cup. He waited until the ball was hit. I think he went the right way every time, but the pace of the ball just beat him. My theory is you've got to guess which way it's going to go and then make your move."

⭐ **But you're not going to reveal all your penalty-saving secrets, are you?**
"Ha, ha, ha! No! I've kept them secret for a long time, so I won't let them slip now!"

⭐ **In a strange way, do you enjoy penalty shoot-outs at the end of big games?**
"Oh yeah, it's a great chance for goalkeepers to become heroes! It's a chance for us to get the glory!

THE SPOT!

CITY and *ENGLAND* legend *DAVID SEAMAN*, who's played in his fair share of nail-biting games!

CHANCE TO BE A HERO!

SEAMO tells MATCH about some of the biggest penalty shoot-outs he's ever taken part in!

ENGLAND v SPAIN
1996 EURO CHAMPIONSHIPS

"When it went to penalties I was really looking forward to it, because we were already on such a roll in the tournament! Spain missed their first penalty so the pressure was on them, and I was lucky enough to make the save that put us through to the semi-final. For a split second I didn't know what had happened, but then I got up and saw everyone cheering and all the lads running at me. I knew we'd won it then!"

ENGLAND v GERMANY
1996 EURO CHAMPIONSHIPS

"That result was hard for us to take, because it knocked us out of the tournament at the semi-final stage when we'd been doing really well. I got my hand to one of them, but the German players all took very good penalties. Actually, all of our penalties were good apart from one – the one that was saved! That was frustrating, but you can't go through life having highs all the time – you've got to experience the lows as well."

ENGLAND v ARGENTINA
1998 WORLD CUP

"I'd made a save early on from one of their guys, and after that Incey stepped up for us. It's so important to score after a save's been made but we didn't, so then we were a bit down. It came to our last penalty and I was having a look around, wondering who was going to take it. I saw David Batty walking up and thought, 'I've never seen him take one in training'. And that was it – he missed and the game was over."

You're not expected to save them and if it goes in, then people always say it was a great penalty! I'd imagine it's the closest feeling we'll ever get to what a striker feels when he scores. So saving a penalty can be a great feeling, but I've been on the other end of it, when you lose the shoot-out, and that can be very cruel."

⭐ What's the atmosphere like before a penalty shoot-out?

"It's a hard time for the players. People ask if we practise taking or saving penalties in training, and we do sometimes – at club and international level. But you can never recreate the tension and the pressure of being out on the pitch when the manager comes up and says, 'Who wants to take one, then?'."

⭐ And the players are usually tired at the end of extra-time...

"Yeah, that's true. Players can often be very tired – that's another reason why you can't practise penalties in training and get a realistic situation. There's tension, there's tiredness and of course there's a lot of pressure on their shoulders. There are thousands of people watching you in the stadium and probably millions watching around the world as well."

⭐ Is the list of takers decided before the game kicks off?

"Sometimes, but what about if a player gets injured during the match? At the end of the day, the players have got to put their hand up and say, 'Yeah, I'll take one,' and that takes a lot of courage when they're in a big game with a lot riding on the outcome. So really you have to decide at the end of the game."

⭐ Finally Seamo, have you ever taken a penalty yourself?

"Yeah, I took a penalty against Manchester United in the 1993 Charity Shield, but I missed! Well, Peter Schmeichel saved it actually! I don't think I'll take one again, I'll stick to saving them from now on!"

Raul and the Real boys have a quick group hug!

fourth XI

Real Madrid 'ave a well wickedy team, but how much do ya know about da Spanish giants?

1 At which famous footy stadium do Real Madrid play their home games?

2 How much did the club pay Juventus to sign Zinedine Zidane in 2001 – £38 million or £48 million?

3 And what number shirt does the ace midfielder wear for the champions of Spain?

4 Which current Real star is the club's top scorer of all time?

5 How many times have they won the European Cup – is it a) 9, b) 10 or c) 11?

6 Which round did Real reach in the 2002-03 Champions League before losing to Juventus?

7 Which England star moved from Merseyside giants Liverpool to Real Madrid in 1999?

8 Which national team does Real's top young goalkeeper Iker Casillas play for?

9 Which popular Spanish team are Real Madrid's main rivals in La Liga?

10 True or false? Real Madrid have never won the UEFA Cup in over 100 years of existence.

11 Which Real Madrid and Cameroon star spent a season on loan at Middlesbrough during the 2002-03 season?

1 POINT PER CORRECT ANSWER

FREAK OR UNIQUE!

True or false? Freddie Ljungberg's purple stripe on his barnet is actually a birthmark.

3 POINTS FOR CORRECT ANSWER

KIT KINGS

Wot unlucky team used to play in this mingin' old kit a few years back?

4 POINTS FOR CORRECT ANSWER

SPOT THE DIFFERENCE!

Are ya sharp enough to spot five differences between these pics?

2 POINTS PER CORRECT ANSWER (MAXIMUM 10)

player match-up

Use yer brains to work out wot international teams these dudes play for!

1. Alessandro Nesta	A. Holland
2. Didi Hamann	B. Norway
3. Eirik Bakke	C. South Africa
4. Kevin Hofland	D. Germany
5. Shaun Bartlett	E. Italy

2 POINTS PER CORRECT ANSWER (MAXIMUM 10)

ONE OF A KIND

Cross out the letters wot appear more than once to reveal da flashy footy star!

**B S M K X C
R X D L M W
A K W D O B**

3 POINTS FOR CORRECT ANSWER

SAY WHAT?

Who is Sir Alex Ferguson talking about here?

IT IS TOTALLY OUT OF THE QUESTION. THERE IS NO WAY WE WOULD SELL HIM OR ANY OF OUR BEST PLAYERS!

2 POINTS FOR CORRECT ANSWER

CAP IN HAND

Eric Cantona woz wicked, but how many times did he play for France?

a) 40
b) 45
c) 99

5 POINTS FOR CORRECT ANSWER

NAFF NOSES!

This one's well tuff! Can you lot work out which players these hooters belong to?

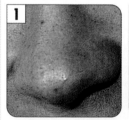
1

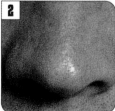
2

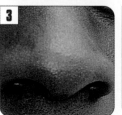
3

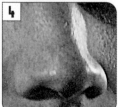
4

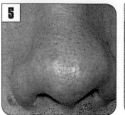
5

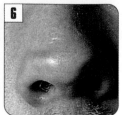
6

2 POINTS PER CORRECT ANSWER (MAXIMUM 12)

MATCH

WORLD SUPERSTARS

Alessandro del Piero ★ Italy

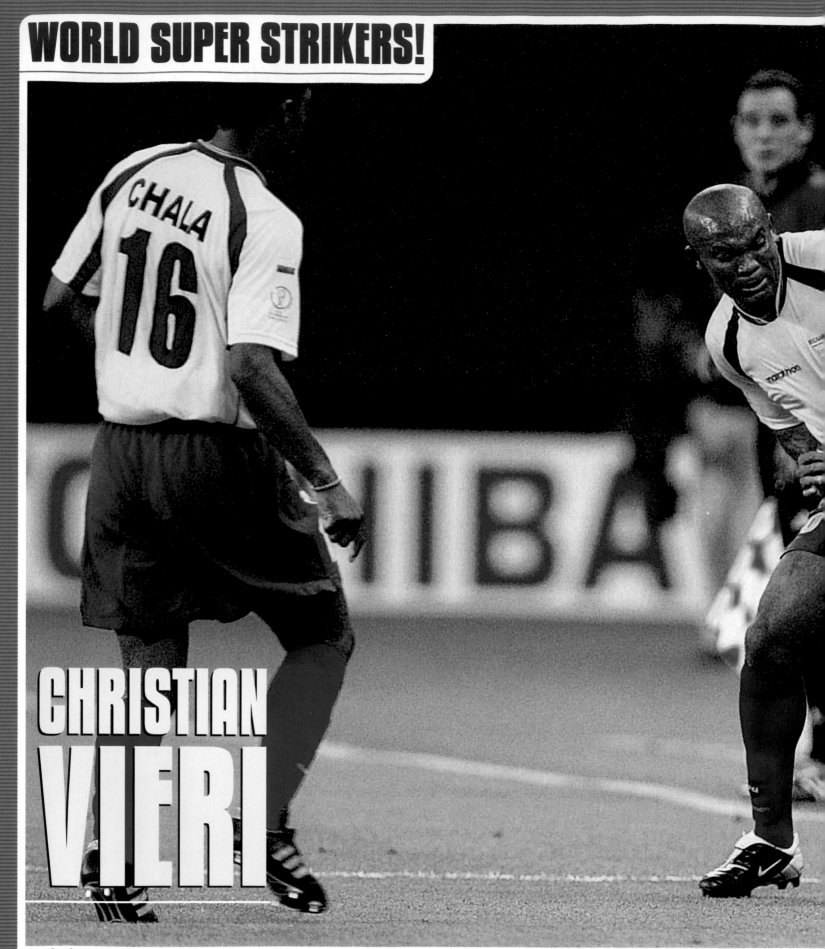

WORLD SUPER STRIKERS!

CHRISTIAN VIERI

Christian Vieri timeline...

July

STAR IS BORN
Vieri is born in Bologna, Italy. His father, Roberto, is a pro who played for many Italian clubs.

1973

December

BACK FROM OZ
Spends most of his childhood in Australia, but returns to Italy. Having loved cricket, he takes up football.

1988

August

TORINO TIME
Plays for Serie C side Prato for a year, then moves to Torino, where he makes his Serie A debut and scores one goal in seven games.

1991

November

ON THE MOVE
Steps down to Serie B side Pisa, then begins to change clubs regularly, moving on to Ravenna, Venezia and Atalanta.

1992

June 1996

JUVE ACE
Signs for mighty Juventus and makes an impact as the Turin side win Serie A.

1996

March

AZZURRI DEBUT
Makes history on his Italy debut, scoring the national team's 1,000th goal in a World Cup qualifier against Moldova.

1997

July

VIVA ESPANA
Arrives in Spanish football with Atletico Madrid. He scores 24 goals to finish the season as La Liga's top scorer.

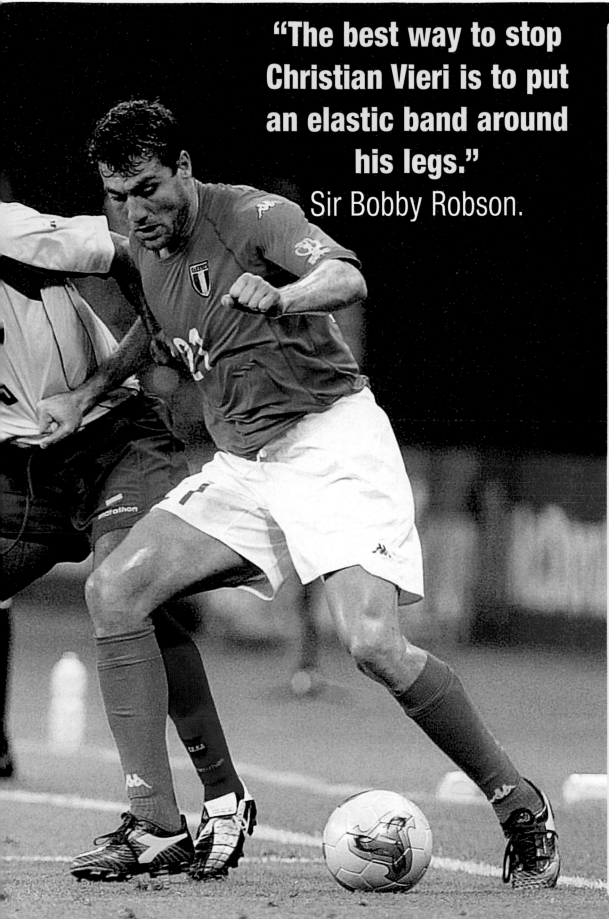

"The best way to stop Christian Vieri is to put an elastic band around his legs."
Sir Bobby Robson.

MATCH charts the rise of INTER MILAN ace CHRISTIAN VIERI!

Christian Vieri's childhood friends used to call him 'Il Mostro' – which means 'The Monster' in Italian – because he couldn't stand still when he was young. And it's a name that has stuck with Vieri, because as he's moved from club to club, he's become a beast of a goalscorer!

His story isn't one of complete success. Born in Italy but raised in Australia after spending most of his childhood in Oz, Vieri had a strange start to his footy career – barely spending longer than one season with a team before moving on for another big transfer fee. He's had his share of injuries too – missing Euro 2000 and last season's vital Champions League semi-final against AC Milan. Vieri's also got a reputation for being moody, after threatening to never celebrate a goal again if the crowd didn't start treating him better!

But he's still one of the best strikers in the world – with a great shot, deceptive pace, the heart of a lion, and the power and build of a heavyweight boxer. Here's the amazing story of how the Italian stallion made it to the top!

CAREER FACTFILE

Born: July 12, 1973 in Bologna

Nationality: Italian

Position: Striker

Height: 6ft 1ins

Weight: 12st 9lbs

Former clubs: Prato, Torino, Pisa, Ravenna, Venezia, Atalanta, Juventus, Atletico Madrid, Lazio

Signed: From Lazio for £31 million on June 10, 1999

Inter debut: v Verona on August 29, 1999 (Serie A)

Total Inter games/goals: 117/84 (August 1999 to May 2003)

International caps/goals: 31/17 (March 1997 to March 2003)

June
WORLD CUP CLASS
Enhances his reputation with five goals in four games for Italy at the 1998 World Cup in France.

August
GO LAZIO
Quits Atletico and returns to Italy with Lazio for £19 million, a record fee for an Italian footballer.

1998

May
EURO KINGS
Misses out on the title by a point but Lazio still win the Cup-Winners' Cup and Vieri scores in the final.

1999

June
RECORD BREAKER
Becomes the most expensive player in the world when Inter Milan sign him for £31 million.

August
TAKE HAT
Makes a sensational Inter debut, scoring a hat-trick against Verona in just over an hour.

June
INJURY
Misses Euro 2000 tournament with a hamstring injury. Italy lose the final to France.

2000

May
TON UP
Plays his 100th Serie A game in January against Parma, then scores his 100th Serie A goal against Atalanta in May.

2001

May
PIPPED AT POST
Loses the title on the last day of the season after defeat at former club Lazio. Another of his old clubs, Juventus, win the Serie A title.

2002

June
CONTROVERSY
Scores in the second round of the World Cup against South Korea, but Italy lose on the Golden Goal rule and go home early.

2003

May
TOP SCORER
Finishes the season as Serie A's leading scorer with 24 goals. But Inter end up without a trophy again.

1996

HAVE GOALS, WILL TRAVEL!

A late developer in football, Vieri moved to Australia aged just four when his dad signed for Oz side Marconi, and he preferred cricket until he was 14! Christian's big break came with Serie C side Prato once his family returned to Italy. Without playing a game, he was picked up by top-flight side Torino – where he scored once in seven appearances. After that, the young striker became a bit of a journeyman, playing for four clubs in four seasons. He played for Serie B clubs Pisa, Ravenna and Venezia between 1992 and 1995. After hitting 11 goals in 29 matches for Venezia, he joined Serie A side Atalanta. And seven goals in 19 games there tempted the mighty Juventus to snap him up in the summer of 1996!

1997

JUVE TITLE JOY!

Vieri had a big job on his hands when he joined Juventus. They had just won the European Cup, he was replacing Gianluca Vialli, and Alen Boksic and Alessandro Del Piero were ahead of him in the pecking order. But he finished the season with a respectable total of eight goals in 23 games as Juventus won the league, and he caught the eye in the European Cup. Cup holders Juve were surprisingly beaten 3-1 by Dortmund in the final though, and Vieri, who started the game only to be replaced in the 70th minute, couldn't prevent the defeat.

> "Bobo is one of the most complete strikers in world football. His pace will always give his team a chance to score."
>
> Filippo Inzaghi

1998

MAY VIERI REIGNS IN SPAIN!

After a successful season at Juve, it was a shock to see Vieri on the move again in the summer of 1997. Despite the protests of Juve chief Giovanni Agnelli, the striker went to Atletico Madrid for £12.5 million before the 1997-98 season started. But the fuss didn't bother Vieri, who enjoyed the most prolific campaign of his career so far – banging home 24 goals in 24 La Liga matches. He was the leading scorer in Spain, even though Atletico only finished fifth in the league, and starred in Europe again. The Italian scored five goals – including strikes against Leicester City and Aston Villa in the UEFA Cup – as Atletico reached the semi-finals. John Gregory, the Villa manager, was keen on signing Vieri but didn't stand a chance! After a single season in Spain, 'Bobo' had become one of the world's most in-demand strikers!

1998

JUNE ON TOP OF THE WORLD!

Vieri went to the 1998 World Cup in France in the form of his life! After his brilliant season in Spain, he was the spearhead of Italy's attack – even though he'd only made his full Italian debut in March 1997 and had a total of just eight caps. But he scored a vital goal in qualifying – in the play-off in Russia – and overshadowed the likes of Del Piero and Roberto Baggio in the finals. He scored in the opening match against Chile, hit two against Cameroon and one each against Austria and Norway. He fired a blank against France in the quarter-finals as Italy lost a penalty shoot-out, but his tally of four goals from five games was only beaten by six-goal Croatian Davor Suker.

1998

JULY LAZIO & SVEN!

Vieri's value shot up again after the World Cup and Atletico couldn't hang on to him. Christian denied rumours of a bust-up with Madrid's new coach Arrigo Saachi, but he still left Spain and returned home to Italy with Lazio. The fee was a whopping £19 million and Vieri was delighted. "I wanted to return and was lucky enough Lazio was interested," he said. "They're a great team and were the club keenest to have me." Linking up with coach Sven Goran Eriksson, the striker was hampered by a knee injury early on, but he showed his true class when he returned, hitting 12 goals in 22 games as the Rome club were pipped to the championship by Milan, by a single point! Consolation came in the form of the European Cup-Winners' Cup, where Lazio lifted the 1999 trophy by beating Real Mallorca 2-1 at Villa Park. Vieri scored Lazio's first and finished the season on a real high note!

1999

INTER THE GROOVE!

After his promising opening season with Lazio, Vieri was expected to stay put in Rome – but it wasn't to be. In the summer of 1999, Inter Milan owner Massimo Moratti happily told the world: "Vieri is Inter's! He will play with Ronaldo next season!" And so he did – after a huge world record transfer fee of £31 million took Vieri from Lazio to Inter – his ninth different club in just eight seasons! He linked up with the brilliant Brazilian Ronaldo under coach Marcelo Lippi, the man whom Christian had played under during his single season with Juventus. "This is the umpteenth time I've moved, but this time I hope to stick around for a while!" Vieri smiled. "I have a five-year deal and I really want to fulfil it, because I don't want to move around any more." His first season was steady, but not spectacular. Vieri scored 12 times in 20 league games as Inter finished fourth and lost the Coppa Italia final. But more bad times were just around the corner for the striker!

2000

OUT OF EURO 2000!

Much like strike partner Ronaldo, Vieri began to spend more time on the treatment table than the pitch. His first season with Inter ended with a hamstring problem, and he didn't recover in time to make Italy's squad for the Euro 2000 championships. But Italy almost won it without him – only losing to France's Golden Goal in the final. Would Vieri have made the difference? We'll never know, but when he returned to action, he wasn't happy. After scoring against Parma in January 2001, he turned his back to the crowd in protest at fans who jeered him. "It's not fair to barrack a player who has been out for nearly ten months," he said. He ended the season with 18 league goals, but his future with Inter was in doubt.

2002

MAY SO CLOSE TO GLORY!

Despite Inter's disappointing 2000-01 season – when they finished fifth, and there was talk of Vieri's return to Juventus – the Italian Stallion stayed at the San Siro and played his part in Inter's title challenge. With Hector Cuper now in charge, Inter were playing well, and although Ronaldo made a tentative return from injury, it was Vieri who led the way with 22 league goals from 25 matches. Inter were in top spot going into the final day, but they fell apart at Lazio, losing 4-2. Juve won their match and leapt over them, and because of Roma's result, Inter eventually finished in third place.

2002

JUNE AN UNHAPPY WORLD CUP!

Vieri didn't have long to mope about Inter's Scudetto disaster, as barely a month later he travelled to South Korea & Japan for the 2002 World Cup. Italy, with much of the squad which went so close to winning Euro 2000, were expected to be serious challengers, and it started well. Vieri scored twice to beat Ecuador in the opening game, and when he put Italy 1-0 ahead against Croatia, The Azzurri were coasting. But Croatia came back to win 2-1 and Italy only made the second round thanks to a nervy 1-1 draw with Mexico. Then came South Korea. Vieri's fourth goal of the tournament gave Italy the lead, but after the hosts levelled, he missed a real sitter which cost his team dear. The Koreans won the tie with a dramatic Golden Goal and the Italians suffered one of the biggest shocks in World Cup history.

2003

GOALS GALORE

The 2002-03 season was Vieri's best in Italian football, even though Inter failed to win a trophy again. Ronaldo had been sold to Real Madrid in the summer, but Vieri carried on banging in the goals. Argentina star Hernan Crespo was his new strike partner, and Bobo's goals kept his side in the title hunt until the final few weeks of the campaign – when the team ran out of steam and eventually finished as runners-up behind Juventus. There was further disappointment for Inter when the club was beaten in the last four of the Champions League by city rivals Milan – with Vieri watching from the bench with a knee ligament injury. But at least he had the satisfaction of becoming the first Inter player for 14 years to win the Serie A top scorer award, boasting a tally of 24 goals in 23 games. And he ain't finished yet!

MYSTIC MATCHMAN!

MATCHY rubs his footy-shaped crystal ball to give a glimpse of the game's amazing future!

Biggedy-big up! Mystic MATCHMAN 'ere – I've put on me spooky hood and used me magic football to find out what the future holds for all me wicked footy mates like Wayne Rooney and little Michael Owen. I is a bit of a psychic, ya see, an' I can see what's just around the corner. So why not get yerself in the know by stealin' a cheeky peek at the 2004-05 season! Future-o-rama footy dudes!

August 2004

English footy is back on the map after Sven's heroes win Euro 2004, with hero Wayne Rooney scoring the winner against hosts Portugal in the final! Sven retires, with Sir Alex Ferguson taking over as England gaffer. Everyone's well excited about the start of the European Super League, with English clubs Man. United Allstars, Arsenal, Newcastle, Liverpool and last year's Premiership champions Chelsea all involved in the mix!

September 2004

AC Milan boss Martin O'Neill snaps up striker Thierry Henry, with Andriy Shevchenko heading to Arsenal, but it's Liverpool who set the pace in the Super League. In the Premiership, Blackburn soar to the top with Everton and Spurs chasing!

October 2004

Despite their mega-bucks sponsorship deal with the Fox Sports Network, Man. United Allstars slip down the Super League table after a string of poor performances. And after failing to score for 11 games, Real Madrid sign Patrick Kluivert for £30 million and Robert Pires for £42 million. In the Premiership, Aston Villa are struggling to cope with David O'Leary's six-week spending spree of £198 million. New England boss Fergie axes the entire squad that won Euro 2004 and plays Michael Ricketts up front on his own as England get stuffed 6-0 at home to Jamaica.

November 2004

Arsenal's Italian strike duo of Christian Vieri and Alessandro del Piero are on fire for The Gunners, but Man. United Allstars midfielder Ronaldinho is all over the tabloids after being caught dating each member of Girls Aloud – the world's biggest pop group – in just a single week. Alex Ferguson deliberately fields only five outfield players in his team as England lose 14-1 to minnows New Zealand.

MUCHOS, MUCHOS RUBBISH!

December 2004

Ronaldo's debut pop single, a duet with Gareth Gates, goes straight in at No.1 despite competition from Big Ron Atkinson's cover of 'The Cheeky Song'. Everton top the Premiership table at Christmas thanks to 14 goals in three games from Rooney. And after years of weight training, Newcastle's Jermaine Jenas becomes a WWE Wrestler.

January 2005

Liverpool move into their new Anfield Arena. Man. United Allstars ace Ronaldinho is back in trouble after being spotted snogging Kylie Minogue, just days after splitting up with sister Dannii. Portsmouth gaffer Harry Redknapp signs England's 1966 World Cup hero Geoff Hurst on a free transfer. "He's got a few years left in 'im yet," says Harry.

February 2005

Chelsea boss Gianfranco Zola leads his team up the Super League table. FA officials uncover Fergie's nasty scheme to wreck England when he tries to appoint fellow Scot Alan Hansen as his assistant manager. Gary Lineker takes over.

March 2005

Arsenal's Italian strike force of Vieri and Del Piero refuse to play because Arsenal's shirts aren't tight enough. Having scored just four goals all season in Spain, Real Madrid sign Michael Owen for £85 million.

April 2005

Everton manager Sir David Moyes refuses to release Wayne Rooney for a friendly, leading to a brawl with England boss Gary Lineker. Sunderland gaffer Mick McCarthy is given a vote of confidence from the board, despite getting The Black Cats relegated to Division Three.

May 2005

Inter Milan win the European Super League title and Everton are crowned 2004-05 Premiership champions. Wayne Rooney scoops the Player Of The Season Award, but is unable to collect the trophy as it's past his bed time. Real Madrid go bankrupt and are demoted to the East Madrid Under-12s School League.

THE KNOWLEDGE

BARCELONA!

1 Barcelona were founded in 1899 by a footy-mad Swiss dude called Hans Gamper, who moved to the city and advertised in the local newspaper for some mates to play with! They met up every week, and soon decided to form Barcelona Football Club!

2 Barça founder Hans Gamper was a footy legend and scored 103 goals for the team in their first three years! He was loving his footy so much he changed his name to Juan, so he sounded more Spanish!

3 Barcelona played bitter rivals Real Madrid for the first time in 1905 and beat them 5-2! Since then, Barça have won 16 Primera Liga titles compared to Madrid's 28, but The Catalans have won the Copa Del Rey 24 times to Madrid's 17!

4 Barça's first stadium was The Bonanova Velodrome, before moving to the 35,000 capacity Les Cortes Stadium in 1922. The Nou Camp was built in 1957 and now holds up to 120,000 people – massive!

5 The Nou Camp was part-financed by Barcelona's 100,000 fanatical fans, who were desperate to outdo Real Madrid! And because it was built in 1957, it cost just £1 million to build the whole stadium. Cheap as chips!

6 Seven of the first nine Barcelona coaches were English, national hero Gary Lineker was once their star striker and former England gaffers Terry Venables and Bobby Robson have both managed the club!

7 David Beckham was at the Nou Camp when he was just 12 years old. They weren't going to sign him, though – he won a trip there with the Bobby Charlton Soccer Skills course!

8 Barça won the European Cup for the first time in 1992 after beating Italian side Sampdoria 1-0 in the final at Wembley!

9 Barcelona is in the Catalonia region of Spain – the people there are so proud, they refuse to ruin their shirts with a sponsor!

10 Barça legend Hristo Stoichkov once chased a rabbit off the Nou Camp pitch! Atletico Madrid fans had smuggled it into the ground and released it on the pitch just as he was about to finish his hat-trick. Gutted!

MATCH

WORLD SUPERSTARS

Edgar Davids ★ Holland

BRAD FRIEDEL'S

STARS IN STRIPES!

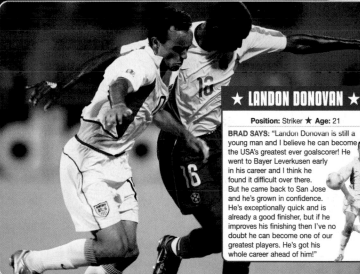

BRAD TELLS MATCH: "After our performance in the 2002 World Cup, I firmly believe the USA can make a real impression in world football in the next few years! Many of our more well-known players, like Claudio Reyna and Chris Armas, probably won't be around at the next World Cup. But we are fortunate to have some outstanding young guys who I'm sure you'll be hearing lots about in the future…"

★ LANDON DONOVAN ★

Position: Striker ★ **Age:** 21

BRAD SAYS: "Landon Donovan is still a young man and I believe he can become the USA's greatest ever goalscorer! He went to Bayer Leverkusen early in his career and I think he found it difficult over there. But he came back to San Jose and he's grown in confidence. He's exceptionally quick and is already a good finisher, but if he improves his finishing then I've no doubt he can become one of our greatest players. He's got his whole career ahead of him!"

★ DAMARCUS BEASLEY ★

Position: Midfielder ★ **Age:** 21

BRAD SAYS: "DaMarcus Beasley is a hot prospect. Like Landon Donovan, he's quick and dangerous, but DaMarcus is different. Landon is a physical player, even though he's small, but DaMarcus uses his pace. He's got a great left foot as well. He's going to be one of those young stars who, if someone in Europe snaps him up, will probably teach him a few things. That advice will help him develop into one of our best players."

★ BRIAN McBRIDE ★

Position: Striker ★ **Age:** 31

BRAD SAYS: "Brian is a good friend, so it was great to see him playing at Everton last season. He's a tall player who is very physical, but he's also got good feet. He's freakishly fit as well, with low body fat levels – he's a natural sportsman, which has helped him become such a good player. Brian's not slow, but he's probably not going to outrun every defender, so he uses his physical presence to great effect on the pitch."

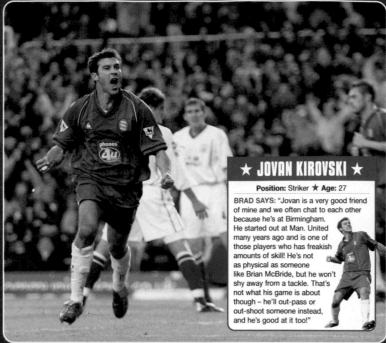

★ JOVAN KIROVSKI ★

Position: Striker ★ **Age:** 27

BRAD SAYS: "Jovan is a very good friend of mine and we often chat to each other because he's at Birmingham. He started out at Man. United many years ago and is one of those players who has freakish amounts of skill! He's not as physical as someone like Brian McBride, but he won't shy away from a tackle. That's not what his game is about though – he'll out-pass or out-shoot someone instead, and he's good at it too!"

★ CLINT MATHIS ★

Position: Striker ★ **Age:** 26

BRAD SAYS: "Clint was at the 2002 World Cup and played a great part in our success over there. He's a goalscorer and a free spirit as well. He's more off-the-wall, more off-the-cuff and more unpredictable than anyone else, and that's a good quality. You don't know what you're going to get from day to day with him – but he'll certainly score goals! He's the type of player who turns games, and that makes him dangerous."

★ PABLO MASTROENI ★

Position: Midfielder ★ **Age:** 27

BRAD SAYS: "For me, Pablo Mastroeni was the highlight of our 2002 World Cup. He probably made it into the team as the 23rd man, because he was called up when Claudio Reyna got injured. But he got a lot of playing time at the World Cup and was probably our most outstanding player. I'm sure people will sit up and take notice of him in the next few years."

★ TEAM ROUND-UP! ★

BRAD SAYS: "The team is looking strong in all areas, and we have some good young players coming through like Kyle Martino. I didn't really know that much about Kyle before Brian McBride spoke to me about him. He plays with Brian at Columbus Crew in the US, and he's been making real waves over there by the sounds of things. Claudio Reyna is really experienced now, but he probably won't make the next World Cup. He was injured last season, but I expect him to bounce back.

Eddie Pope and Earnie Stewart have also been great servants for us, and without them we're going to have to work hard to find replacements. John O'Brien, who's at Ajax, is learning a lot and Joe Max-Moore had a spell in England with Everton. A lot of US players are getting experience of European football now, and we have a lot of good young players who can pick stuff up from these guys – like Bobby Convey at DC United and Nick Garcia at Kansas City Wizards, so the future looks good!"

MATCH

WORLD SUPERSTARS

Roberto Carlos ★ Brazil

50

TOP PREMIERSHIP PLAYERS OF 2002-03!

Wanna know the real stars of last season's Premiership? Now you can check out the top 50 players – exclusively rated by MATCHfacts!

Think back to November last year and you'll remember that Arsenal were flying in the Premiership. Thierry Henry was playing out of his skin and The Gunners were nine points clear of Man. United – who were struggling big time back in fifth place!

But with Roy Keane back to fitness and Ruud van Nistelrooy banging in goals all over the place, The Red Devils came roaring back in the New Year to win their eighth title in 11 seasons! Newcastle and Chelsea clinched the other all-important Champions League places, Thierry Henry was deservedly named the PFA and Football Writers' Player Of The Year, while Ruud van Nistelrooy finished top scorer with 25 league goals.

But which player topped our MATCHfacts ratings? Who performed week in, week out for their club? These are the most accurate ratings you'll find, because we watch every game of the season and we don't rate players by their reputation – they have to earn their mark out of ten every week! Now you can find out who's won our prestigious MATCHMAN Of The Season award, as we count down the 50 best players of the last campaign...

PREVIOUS MATCHMEN OF THE YEAR!

1997-1998	1998-1999	1999-2000	2000-2001	2001-2002
Dennis BERGKAMP *Arsenal*	**Tony ADAMS** *Arsenal*	**Paolo DI CANIO** *West Ham*	**Ryan GIGGS** *Man. United*	**Roy KEANE** *Man. United*

In MATCHfacts, everyone who plays more than 20 minutes in a game is awarded a rating out of ten and the best player of the game is given a star rating. Players must have played at least 19 games in the 2002-03 season to be in the running for the MATCHMAN Of The Season award – the ultimate reward for excellence in every game!

PATRICK VIEIRA
Arsenal

Age: 27 ★ **Position:** Midfielder

Lowdown: Between August and January last season, Arsenal were the most exciting team to watch in Europe – let alone the Premiership! The speed of their attacks had opposing teams gasping for breath and they often finished the game as a contest within 20 minutes! Running the show in midfield was Patrick Vieira, breaking down the opposition with his powerful tackling, then covering the length of the pitch in seconds with his enormous stride before feeding Wiltord, Bergkamp or Henry. He managed to win eight star ratings in 24 games – easily the best record in the Premiership last season – and The Gunners only lost three of their league games in which the Frenchman played.

MATCHFACTS RATINGS		
PLAYED	STARS	AVERAGE
24	8	7.50

> Why did Vieira have such a good season, then?
Well, Arsenal started the campaign on fire, and that helped him to forget about France's disastrous World Cup in the summer. Vieira had been made the club captain after Tony Adams retired and The Gunners went into the new season as champions, so it was an exciting time at Highbury. Gilberto Silva joined to play next to Vieira in midfield, and that allowed the Frenchman to take on a more attacking role, which he relished.

> So how come Arsenal didn't manage to win the title?
After being top of the table for most of the season until April, The Gunners were red-hot favourites to win the Premiership. But Arsene Wenger's men peaked too early, and injuries to David Seaman, Sol Campbell and Vieira himself began to affect the team's results. They were knocked out of the Champions League by Valencia in March and never really recovered, especially when Vieira was ruled out for the season because of a knee injury with five games to go. He also missed Arsenal's FA Cup final win over Southampton in Cardiff.

> What about Paddy's dodgy disciplinary record?
Vieira was only booked five times last season. But he was sent-off for two bookable offences at Chelsea, and then told ref Andy D'Urso he had no personality, which earned him a costly two-game suspension and a £25,000 fine. But the Gunners skipper improved on the season before, proving many critics wrong.

> What can we expect from him in the future?
After pledging his future to Arsenal, big Paddy V wants the title back at Highbury. But that's not going to be an easy task, so he'll have to play even better than last season – and try to avoid injury. Then there's Euro 2004 in the summer, and Vieira will be one of France's big guns as the tournament's defending champions. Paddy still wants to captain his country on a permanent basis, but Marcel Desailly and Zinedine Zidane are in his way at the moment!

THIERRY HENRY
Arsenal

Age: 26 ★ **Position:** Striker

Lowdown: No other player lit up last season's Premiership like Thierry Henry. His slick control and blistering pace caused chaos in opposition defences, and his goals came from all over the pitch – including brilliant solo dribbles, awesome long-range bullets and pinpoint free-kicks. He scored 24 goals and made an incredible 23 assists for his team-mates at Highbury, which makes him the most unselfish striker ever! Titi was also voted the PFA and Football Writers' Player Of The Year. For individual brilliance and sheer entertainment, he was head and shoulders above anyone else in the Premiership. He's now one of the most wanted men in Europe, with an unbelievable price tag of £70 million on his head. So look out for him at Real Madrid next season – even if they deny it!

MATCHFACTS RATINGS		
PLAYED	STARS	AVERAGE
37	6	7.30

3

ROY KEANE
Manchester United

Age: 32 ★ **Position:** Midfielder

Lowdown: It's no coincidence that Man. United came storming back into the title race when their inspirational captain returned from a bad hip injury in December. After losing 3-1 to Middlesbrough on his first game back, the critics had written him off as well past his best – but what followed was 16 games unbeaten until the end of the campaign. The mere presence of Keano lifted his team-mates in the dressing room and it heaped pressure on Arsenal, allowing The Red Devils to bring the Premiership trophy back to Old Trafford.

MATCHFACTS RATINGS		
PLAYED	STARS	AVERAGE
21	3	7.24

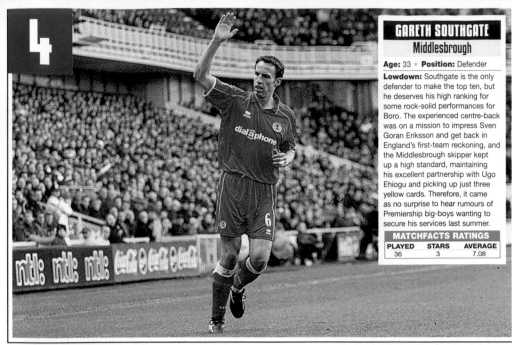

4

5

GARETH SOUTHGATE
Middlesbrough

Age: 33 ★ **Position:** Defender

Lowdown: Southgate is the only defender to make the top ten, but he deserves his high ranking for some rock-solid performances for Boro. The experienced centre-back was on a mission to impress Sven Goran Eriksson and get back in England's first-team reckoning, and the Middlesbrough skipper kept up a high standard, maintaining his excellent partnership with Ugo Ehiogu and picking up just three yellow cards. Therefore, it came as no surprise to hear rumours of Premiership big-boys wanting to secure his services last summer.

MATCHFACTS RATINGS

PLAYED	STARS	AVERAGE
36	3	7.08

PAUL SCHOLES
Manchester United

Age: 28 ★ **Position:** Midfielder

Lowdown: Sir Alex Ferguson's decision to play Scholes behind Ruud van Nistelrooy paid off for Man. United last season. But Van Nistelrooy wouldn't have won the Golden Boot without Paul's clever promptings, sublime touch and razor-sharp brain. He was different class at times, scoring 14 league goals and hitting a hat-trick in the vital 6-2 win at Newcastle in April.

MATCHFACTS RATINGS

PLAYED	STARS	AVERAGE
33	6	7.06

6

DAMIEN DUFF
Blackburn Rovers

Age: 24 ★ **Position:** Midfielder

Lowdown: The dazzling Republic Of Ireland winger had a lot to live up to after his impressive World Cup. A handful for every side he faced in the Premiership, Rovers boss Graeme Souness soon put a multi-million pound price tag on his head. He was right to do it, too – Duffer was their most creative player and top scorer last season, with nine goals from 26 games!

MATCHFACTS RATINGS

PLAYED	STARS	AVERAGE
26	3	7.04

8

JONATHAN GREENING
Middlesbrough

Age: 24 ★ **Position:** Midfielder

Lowdown: It may be a surprise to see Greening in the top ten, but the stats don't lie! He began the season in dazzling form and was rewarded with a call-up to an England get-together in November. The creative midfielder played in all of Boro's 38 Premiership games and he was their star man seven times – the second best record behind Arsenal's Patrick Vieira.

MATCHFACTS RATINGS

PLAYED	STARS	AVERAGE
38	7	7.00

7

KIERON DYER
Newcastle United

Age: 24 ★ **Position:** Midfielder

Lowdown: Dyer was able to play much more of a starring role for Bobby Robson's men last season after an injury-plagued 2001-02 campaign. The 24-year-old star helped Newcastle to third place in the Premiership, sometimes winning games on his own with breathtaking speed and skill. If he can score a few more goals he'll be the perfect attacking midfielder, and Robson reckons he should be playing in the centre for England rather than his current bit-part role!

MATCHFACTS RATINGS

PLAYED	STARS	AVERAGE
35	5	7.03

9

FRANK LAMPARD
Chelsea

Age: 25 ★ **Position:** Midfielder

Lowdown: Lamps is no longer just a young player with potential, as he was at West Ham. He was one of the best midfielders in the country in 2002-03, commanding the centre of the park and offering an important link between defence and attack. He scored six goals for The Blues, won star ratings left, right and centre, and became a regular in the England squad.

MATCHFACTS RATINGS		
PLAYED	STARS	AVERAGE
38	6	6.97

11

JERZY DUDEK
Liverpool

Age: 30 ★ **Position:** Goalkeeper

Lowdown: Dudek can look on his ranking with pride. An infamous clanger against Man. United last December left his Liverpool career on the skids, but after reclaiming the No.1 jersey from the injured Chris Kirkland, the Poland stopper showed his class. Other 'keepers may have received more plaudits than him, but Dudek is the only one to appear in the top 30.

MATCHFACTS RATINGS		
PLAYED	STARS	AVERAGE
30	1	6.93

10

STEVEN GERRARD
Liverpool

Age: 23 ★ **Position:** Midfielder

Lowdown: Stevie G flew out of the traps after missing the World Cup due to a hernia operation, and helped Liverpool to the top of the table. But his form dipped badly in November and he was dropped from the first-team and publicly criticised by boss Gerrard Houllier. The midfielder's response was to knuckle down in training and he soon got back to his best, finishing the season with five goals and an impressive eight assists – most of them being for his deadly England team-mate Michael Owen.

MATCHFACTS RATINGS		
PLAYED	STARS	AVERAGE
34	4	6.97

12

YOURI DJORKAEFF
Bolton Wanderers

Age: 35 ★ **Position:** Striker

Lowdown: As inspired signings go, Djorkaeff tops the lot. Bolton got one of France's leading players of the 1990s for absolutely nothing, and despite celebrating his 35th birthday during the 2002-03 term, his silky skills were key in keeping the Wanderers in the Premiership. His seven league goals were also priceless, not least the one which helped Bolton to a valuable draw against Arsenal at the end of April.

MATCHFACTS RATINGS		
PLAYED	STARS	AVERAGE
36	2	6.92

13

DAVID THOMPSON
Blackburn Rovers

Age: 26 ★ **Position:** Midfielder

Lowdown: Rovers signed David in August 2002 from Coventry and the £1.5 million midfielder made an immediate impact. Competitive and aggressive, but skilful at the same time, he made his mark at Ewood Park with goals against Chelsea, Man. City and CSKA Sofia, and even made the England squad. He failed to win a cap, but impressed before injury struck.

MATCHFACTS RATINGS		
PLAYED	STARS	AVERAGE
23	6	6.91

14

DIETMAR HAMANN
Liverpool

Age: 30 ★ **Position:** Midfielder

Lowdown: Hamann rarely grabs the headlines, but last season he was still a vital cog in Liverpool's midfield. The German's speciality is winning the ball and distributing it simply – and his team-mates appreciated his performances in the 30 Premiership appearances he made. Hamann also scored two goals in 2002-03, with strikes against Newcastle and Fulham.

MATCHFACTS RATINGS		
PLAYED	STARS	AVERAGE
30	3	6.90

15

TUGAY
Blackburn Rovers

Age: 33 ★ **Position:** Midfielder

Lowdown: Tugay was in superb form as he helped Rovers to sixth place in the 2002-03 Premiership. The Turkish ace was a tower of strength for Blackburn in a deep midfield role, sweeping up in front of the defence and launching many attacks with his excellent passing. The fiery side of his game was kept largely under control, apart from his sending-off at Southampton, and his one goal was memorable last season – coming in the 2-0 home win against Arsenal in March.

MATCHFACTS RATINGS		
PLAYED	STARS	AVERAGE
37	6	6.89

16

JONATHAN WOODGATE
Newcastle United

Age: 23 ★ **Position:** Defender

Lowdown: Woody broke the hearts of Leeds fans when he left for Newcastle in January 2003. He had been brilliant in the first half of the season at Elland Road before The Magpies paid £9 million for his services. Despite playing just ten matches for Newcastle through injury, Woodgate showed enough quality to suggest he'll be a long-term success at St James' Park.

MATCHFACTS RATINGS		
PLAYED	STARS	AVERAGE
28	1	6.89

17

GIANFRANCO ZOLA
Chelsea

Age: 37 ★ **Position:** Striker

Lowdown: Zola defied the odds – and his age – to produce a series of top performances in 2002-03. The Italian was expected to play just a cameo role but made 30 starts and featured in every league game. All his traditional qualities – quick vision, neat feet and curling free-kicks – were there for all to see, and with 14 goals he finished as Chelsea's leading goalscorer.

MATCHFACTS RATINGS		
PLAYED	STARS	AVERAGE
38	5	6.87

18

GUDNI BERGSSON
Bolton Wanderers

Age: 38 ★ **Position:** Defender

Lowdown: Bergsson is a Bolton legend after eight years with the club, and he was excellent again in his last season – finally retiring after helping The Trotters to safety. The Icelandic defender was a rock of consistency in Bolton's back four, where his mistakes could have been counted on one hand. Wanderers will miss him, and will find him very difficult to replace.

MATCHFACTS RATINGS		
PLAYED	STARS	AVERAGE
31	1	6.87

19

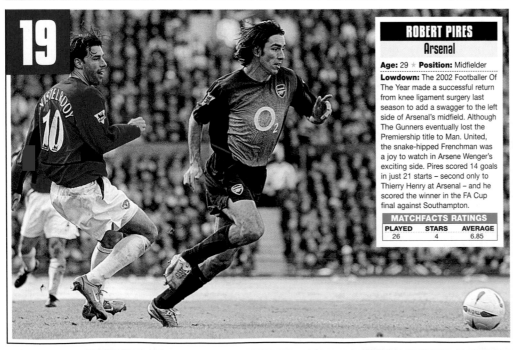

ROBERT PIRES
Arsenal

Age: 29 ★ **Position:** Midfielder

Lowdown: The 2002 Footballer Of The Year made a successful return from knee ligament surgery last season to add a swagger to the left side of Arsenal's midfield. Although The Gunners eventually lost the Premiership title to Man. United, the snake-hipped Frenchman was a joy to watch in Arsene Wenger's exciting side. Pires scored 14 goals in just 21 starts – second only to Thierry Henry at Arsenal – and he scored the winner in the FA Cup final against Southampton.

MATCHFACTS RATINGS		
PLAYED	STARS	AVERAGE
26	4	6.85

20

SOL CAMPBELL
Arsenal

Age: 29 ★ **Position:** Defender

Lowdown: It was a shame Sol missed the climax of the season through suspension, because until his red card against Man. United in April he'd been a giant at the heart of Arsenal's defence. Extra responsibility was thrust his way after Tony Adams left, but Sol took it all in his stride. When he was banned for the final few matches, The Gunners looked vulnerable.

MATCHFACTS RATINGS		
PLAYED	STARS	AVERAGE
33	0	6.85

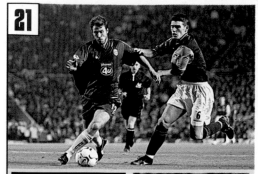

21

KENNY CUNNINGHAM
Birmingham City

Age: 32 ★ **Position:** Defender

Lowdown: With Birmingham gaffer Steve Bruce needing an experienced defender to lead The Blues in their debut Premiership season, he moved for Wimbledon star Cunningham in the summer of 2002. Kenny quickly settled into the heart of defence and was even named captain after his consistent performances. One booking from 31 games proves how tidy he was.

MATCHFACTS RATINGS		
PLAYED	STARS	AVERAGE
31	2	6.84

22

CRAIG BELLAMY
Newcastle United

Age: 24 ★ **Position:** Striker

Lowdown: Wales international Bellamy always seemed to be hitting the headlines in 2002-03. Tendinitis in his knees restricted his performances at the beginning of the season, but he returned to the side in style with a second-minute goal against rivals Sunderland. His partnership with Alan Shearer was among the best in the country, and his energetic displays and committed attitude is loved by the Newcastle fans. But he needs to curb his temper, as he was sent-off twice in the Champions League.

MATCHFACTS RATINGS		
PLAYED	STARS	AVERAGE
29	4	6.83

23

GEREMI
Middlesbrough

Age: 24 ★ **Position:** Midfielder

Lowdown: Steve McClaren was well pleased when he secured Geremi on loan from Real Madrid in the summer of 2002. The classy Cameroon midfielder soon became a permanent fixture on the right of Boro's midfield and his inspirational displays and great goals – like his stunning free-kick against Liverpool – meant the club were desperate to hang on to him permanently. It's hard to believe he's still only 24!

MATCHFACTS RATINGS		
PLAYED	STARS	AVERAGE
33	3	6.82

24

CLAUS LUNDEKVAM
Southampton

Age: 30 ★ **Position:** Defender

Lowdown: Nicknamed 'Silky' by his Southampton team-mates for his ability on the ball, the Norway international is one of the league's most under-rated players. Strong in the air and a good reader of the game, Lundekvam's composed displays helped The Saints to their impressive eighth-place finish and a runners-up spot to Arsenal in last season's FA Cup final.

MATCHFACTS RATINGS		
PLAYED	STARS	AVERAGE
33	0	6.82

25

SEAN DAVIS
Fulham

Age: 24 ★ **Position:** Midfielder

Lowdown: The 2002-03 season was, amazingly, Sean's seventh professional campaign with the club. He impressed again with his all-action midfield displays and collected five star ratings from his 28 Premiership games. In fact, he was so hot he got called up to the full England squad for the friendly with Australia in February and was unlucky not to get off the bench.

MATCHFACTS RATINGS		
PLAYED	STARS	AVERAGE
28	5	6.82

26

EYAL BERKOVIC
Manchester City

Age: 31 ★ **Position:** Midfielder

Lowdown: The little Israeli wizard was a key man in City's return to the Premiership, and in 2002-03 he did more than enough to earn a place in the team. Battling with City's other creative midfielder Ali Benarbia, Eyal started 27 games and made eight assists – one more than Benarbia. Said to be unhappy at the club for much of last season, he still had a successful campaign for Kevin Keegan's boys.

MATCHFACTS RATINGS		
PLAYED	STARS	AVERAGE
27	3	6.81

27

JASON KOUMAS
West Bromwich Albion

Age: 24 ★ **Position:** Midfielder

Lowdown: Koumas moved to West Brom in August 2002 after catching the eye with Tranmere. While the attacking midfielder wasn't able to stop The Baggies dropping into Division One, he was still their star man with six assists, back-to-back goals against Villa and Sunderland, and a fine strike against Man. United. Deserves to be back playing in the top flight!

MATCHFACTS RATINGS		
PLAYED	STARS	AVERAGE
32	2	6.81

28

AARON HUGHES
Newcastle United

Age: 23 ★ **Position:** Defender

Lowdown: The Northern Ireland international continued to make the Newcastle right-back position his own in 2002-03, clocking up more appearances than any other defender at the North-East club. A big part of his game is driving forward down the wing, and he made an impressive 45 crosses last season to set up numerous chances for his team-mates.

MATCHFACTS RATINGS		
PLAYED	STARS	AVERAGE
35	0	6.80

29

JAMES BEATTIE
Southampton

Age: 25 ★ **Position:** Striker

Lowdown: Beattie started the 2002-03 season slowly, failing to score in his first nine games – but he finished in fine form, with 23 league goals and England caps too! The former Blackburn trainee quickly became England's hottest striker thanks to his eye for goal, and he scored everything from simple tap-ins to amazing 30-yard screamers. His ability to hit the net consistently earned him a deserved England debut in February and a new, improved Saints contract.

MATCHFACTS RATINGS		
PLAYED	STARS	AVERAGE
38	6	6.79

30

LAUREN
Arsenal

Age: 26 ★ **Position:** Defender

Lowdown: Dependable Lauren enjoyed another solid season for the 2002-03 Premiership runners-up. Although not as dynamic as in the title-winning campaign the year before, the right-back still loved to link up with the forwards and scored against West Brom and Birmingham. A total of six yellow cards definitely gives him something to improve on, though.

MATCHFACTS RATINGS		
PLAYED	STARS	AVERAGE
27	0	6.78

31

TOMASZ RADZINSKI
Everton

Age: 29 ★ **Position:** Striker

Lowdown: If you believe all the hype, there was only one striker playing for Everton last season. But while Wayne Rooney grabbed all the headlines, Tomasz Radzinski shrugged off an indifferent first Premiership season to prove how dangerous he can be. Fast, tricky and with a good eye for goal, the Canadian striker bagged 11 goals last season to top the Everton scoring charts. Wayne who?

MATCHFACTS RATINGS		
PLAYED	STARS	AVERAGE
30	3	6.77

32

THOMAS GRAVESEN
Everton

Age: 27 ★ **Position:** Midfielder

Lowdown: Following a promising showing at the 2002 World Cup, Danish enforcer Gravesen enjoyed another consistent season with The Toffees. His all-action style makes him a big favourite with the Everton faithful, and the 11 yellow cards he picked up last season proves he isn't afraid to get stuck in. But Thomas can play a bit too, as six assists in 2002-03 proves.

MATCHFACTS RATINGS		
PLAYED	STARS	AVERAGE
33	3	6.76

33

DENNIS BERGKAMP
Arsenal

Age: 34 ★ **Position:** Striker

Lowdown: Bergkamp seems to be a permanent fixture in MATCH's 50 Best Players line-up, and he's made it here thanks to his consistent displays last season. He wasn't as dazzling as usual – failing to pick up any star ratings in 29 games – but his classy play took Arsenal close to keeping their Premiership crown and helped them lift the FA Cup in Cardiff.

MATCHFACTS RATINGS		
PLAYED	STARS	AVERAGE
29	0	6.76

34

JOHN TERRY
Chelsea

Age: 22 ★ **Position:** Defender

Lowdown: Equally as happy putting in a bone-crunching tackle as bringing the ball out of defence and spraying a 50-yard pass, John Terry's contribution was huge last season for Chelsea, and England honours can't be too far away.

MATCHFACTS RATINGS		
PLAYED	STARS	AVERAGE
20	2	6.75

35

SAMI HYYPIA
Liverpool

Age: 29 ★ **Position:** Defender

Lowdown: The Liverpool skipper only missed two games last term and was a model defender with his solid style. Unfortunately, fellow defender Stephane Henchoz was injured for long spells which didn't help The Reds' title ambitions.

MATCHFACTS RATINGS		
PLAYED	STARS	AVERAGE
36	1	6.75

36

MARCEL DESAILLY
Chelsea

Age: 35 ★ **Position:** Defender

Lowdown: The World Cup winner might be knocking on a bit, but he showed in 2002-03 that he still sets the standards by which others follow. Despite the emergence of John Terry, Desailly kept the young star on the sidelines for much of last season as he helped Chelsea to a Champions League spot in the last game against Liverpool. Still looks class at the age of 35!

MATCHFACTS RATINGS		
PLAYED	STARS	AVERAGE
31	0	6.74

37

WILLIAM GALLAS
Chelsea

Age: 26 ★ **Position:** Defender

Lowdown: When you have to play alongside French legend Marcel Desailly in defence, there's always a danger that you'll look poor in comparison – but that isn't the case for William Gallas. If anything, the defender often overshadowed his fellow countryman with some fantastic displays for The Blues during 2002-03. An ever-present in the league, he helped Chelsea qualify for the Champions League and was rewarded by being named in the PFA Team Of The Year.

MATCHFACTS RATINGS		
PLAYED	STARS	AVERAGE
38	2	6.74

RUUD VAN NISTELROOY
Manchester United

Age: 27 ★ **Position:** Striker

Lowdown: It's a surprise to see Ruud van Nistelrooy here in 38th place – especially as he scored 25 goals in last season's Premiership! But Ruud didn't get off to the best start in 2002-03 and this top 50 is based on the players' consistency over the whole season! At his best, the Dutchman was aweome, and after scoring 13 goals in his last eight league games, Ruud won the Golden Boot. More importantly, he won his first Man. United trophy since joining the club in 2001!

MATCHFACTS RATINGS		
PLAYED	STARS	AVERAGE
34	2	6.74

39

SHAY GIVEN
Newcastle United

Age: 27 ★ **Position:** Goalkeeper

Lowdown: The fact that no-one remembers Newcastle reserve 'keeper Steve Harper says it all about Shay Given. The Irishman was an ever-present last season, which meant all Harper caught was a cold from sitting on the bench! Given had his work cut out behind an uncertain defence, but his steady form helped the club to another Champions League place.

MATCHFACTS RATINGS		
PLAYED	STARS	AVERAGE
38	0	6.74

40

CARLO CUDICINI
Chelsea

Age: 30 ★ **Position:** Goalkeeper

Lowdown: You know you've had a good season if you're an Italian but you get tipped for a call-up to the England squad! That was the situation that Carlo Cudicini – who will soon qualify for the Three Lions after playing in England for five years – found himself in. The Chelsea 'keeper was inspirational last term and just missed out on making the PFA Team Of The Year.

MATCHFACTS RATINGS		
PLAYED	STARS	AVERAGE
36	2	6.72

41

WAYNE BRIDGE
Southampton

Age: 23 ★ **Position:** Defender

Lowdown: Bridgey's work-rate and ability to get forward played a key part in The Saints' success last season as they finished eighth in the Premiership. The 23-year-old is now pushing Ashley Cole hard for the England left-back spot.

MATCHFACTS RATINGS		
PLAYED	STARS	AVERAGE
34	2	6.71

42

GILBERTO SILVA
Arsenal

Age: 26 ★ **Position:** Midfielder

Lowdown: World Cup-winning midfielder Gilberto Silva joined The Gunners from Brazilian side Atletico Mineiro in a £4.5 million switch last season and made an immediate impact – scoring the winning goal in the FA Community Shield. Since then his partnership with Vieira has flourished, and with some help from fellow Brazilian Edu, Gilberto settled in quickly and made a big impression in England during his first Premiership season.

MATCHFACTS RATINGS		
PLAYED	STARS	AVERAGE
35	0	6.71

43

JAY-JAY OKOCHA
Bolton Wanderers

Age: 30 ★ **Position:** Midfielder

Lowdown: After taking some time to adjust to the Premiership's pace after joining from PSG, Jay-Jay became the league's top trickster and played a key role in saving The Trotters from the dreaded drop with his magical skill and ability.

MATCHFACTS RATINGS		
PLAYED	STARS	AVERAGE
31	3	6.71

44

GARY SPEED
Newcastle United

Age: 33 ★ **Position:** Midfielder

Lowdown: Gary Speed showed that age was no barrier by securing a regular place in one of the most talented midfields in the country in 2002-03. With players like Dyer, Jenas, Viana, Robert and Solano all competing for places, Magpies gaffer Bobby Robson was spoilt for choice – but he still plumped for experience by picking Speed when fit. His faith was repaid, as Speed's leadership and work-rate helped The Toon to a Champions League place for a second season running.

MATCHFACTS RATINGS
PLAYED	STARS	AVERAGE
24	1	6.71

45

DARREN PURSE
Birmingham City

Age: 26 ★ **Position:** Defender

Lowdown: Darren Purse was sorely missed in the centre of Birmingham's defence last year. Purse picked up an infection after an ankle operation which kept him out for four months. But despite making only 20 Premiership starts, the robust centre-back did enough to convince gaffer Steve Bruce that he's an important part of the revolution at St Andrews.

MATCHFACTS RATINGS
PLAYED	STARS	AVERAGE
20	1	6.70

46

HUGO VIANA
Newcastle United

Age: 20 ★ **Position:** Midfielder

Lowdown: After arriving from Sporting Lisbon for £8.5 million, the Portuguese wonderkid was hailed as 'Newcastle's Wayne Rooney' by Kieron Dyer. He had more shots on target last season than Jermaine Jenas, created the same number of goals as Laurent Robert and scored two goals in his last two Premiership games. He's definitely one for the future!

MATCHFACTS RATINGS
PLAYED	STARS	AVERAGE
23	0	6.70

47

GARETH BARRY
Aston Villa

Age: 22 ★ **Position:** Midfielder

Lowdown: Bazza prospered in his switch to midfield last season, which led to a deserved England call-up in the summer. The classy Villa ace made six goals, hit 94 crosses from his new left-wing spot and scored three goals.

MATCHFACTS RATINGS
PLAYED	STARS	AVERAGE
35	5	6.69

48

LUCAS NEILL
Blackburn Rovers

Age: 25 ★ **Position:** Defender

Lowdown: The Aussie star made a big impression last season and his versatility proved useful for Rovers, with no outfield player starting more games. Playing mainly at right-back, Neill made 71 crosses and three assists.

MATCHFACTS RATINGS
PLAYED	STARS	AVERAGE
34	0	6.68

49

ASHLEY COLE
Arsenal

Age: 22 ★ **Position:** Defender

Lowdown: Despite missing March because of a hernia operation, Ash continued to develop as one of the best left-backs in the Premiership. The Stepney-born youngster was a regular in Arsenal's back four, and his fine attacking instincts saw him carve out five assists and even sneak a goal against West Brom! Cole also continues to hold down the England left-back spot.

MATCHFACTS RATINGS
PLAYED	STARS	AVERAGE
31	1	6.68

50

DAVID BECKHAM
Manchester United

Age: 28 ★ **Position:** Midfielder

Lowdown: The most famous footy star on the planet only scraped into our top 50 – but Becks finished the season in style with seven goals in his last 12 games for club and country. Becks was vital to United's championship success, creating nine goals and bending in 201 crosses in what proved to be his last season at Old Trafford before his switch to Real Madrid. He'll be sorely missed in the Premiership.

MATCHFACTS RATINGS
PLAYED	STARS	AVERAGE
31	1	6.68

Skipper Roy Keane lifts the league title in 2003.

fifth XI

Man. United won the Premiership last season, but just how much do ya know about them?

1 Which gaffer who's now a footy pundit managed Manchester United before Sir Alex Ferguson took over?

2 From which club did Ferguson sign his influential skipper Roy Keane?

3 Which international team does United midfielder Quinton Fortune play for?

4 How many times have United won the FA Cup – is it a) 8, b) 9 or c) 10?

5 And how many times have The Red Devils won the Premiership title?

6 From which club did Man. United sign Holland striker Ruud van Nistelrooy?

7 True or false? When they were first formed, United were actually called Newton Heath.

8 At which First Division club did Luke Chadwick spend part of the 2002-03 season on loan?

9 True or false? Man. United had to play their home games at Man. City's Maine Road stadium during World War II.

10 Which giant Dutch defender left Old Trafford to join Lazio back in 2001?

11 Which famous former United super striker is now in charge of Wales?

1 POINT PER CORRECT ANSWER

⚽ GROUND FORCE ⚽

Which Premiership team used to play at this well smart ground?

1 POINT FOR CORRECT ANSWER

WHO AM I?

Which mop-topped Arsenal player is tangling with Wes Brown here?

1 POINT FOR CORRECT ANSWER

ALPHABET QUIZ

The answers to all these teasers begin with the letter 'D'. 'Ave it!

1. The surname of baldy Aston Villa and former England striker, Dion.
2. Top European striker Diego Tristan plays for this Spanish side.
3. Middlesbrough signed Chris Riggott and Malcolm Christie from this club.
4. Cat-like Liverpool and Poland 'keeper whose first name is Jerzy.
5. Midfielder Thomas Gravesen plays for this international team.

2 POINTS PER CORRECT ANSWER

GOALMOUTH SCRAMBLE

You need to find 15 words or more from Sol Campbell's surname to get on the scoreboard! Tuff enuff for ya?

L L C A
L · · A
E · · M
E B P

1 POINT PER CORRECT ANSWER (MAXIMUM 15)

CAP IN HAND

Alan Shearer woz well good when he played for England, but how many caps did he win?

a) 63
b) 64
c) 65

1 POINT FOR CORRECT ANSWER

WORD SEARCH

All these geezers are wicked strikers, but you'll need to spot 'em all to get maximum points!

```
V N S R L H N O J Y A L O Z T O T T I
T L B V I Q N I N R V N O S S R A L L
E A C U W A V K J N I B Z Q N K K C T
K L U I V E R T Q Q E P A K L H I B F
X E N O R A C C A M R I R D N V X N B
A A L E D R A J Y F I U O J E L Y A V
N H A S S E L B A I N K N C S F O M I
E H A T E U G E Z E R T A Z A A O Z D
W H O L L I T R O P T V L X V M R E U
O N A T S I R T X S O F D A I I L K K
F D D A G B Y Q D K D I O N O H E H A
X X Y X F N T J S A L A S E L G T R U
S H E V C H E N K O B E R L A A S E R
B A R O S Y D I O U F E P K L Z I R O
R A U L A H E N R Y W X A A M N N A O
X I V A L D N W B J X D K T A I N E N
W S K C I S S E T O R R E S T U A H E
F A D E L P I E R O S M I T H I V S Y
M O I V Q H A R T S O N E E O V E X Q
```

› Anelka	› Kezman	› Saviola
› Baros	› Kluivert	› Shearer
› Beattie	› Kovacevic	› Shevchenko
› Cisse	› Larsson	› Smith
› Defoe	› Maccarone	› Torres
› Del Piero	› Makaay	› Totti
› Diouf	› Owen	› Trezeguet
› Hartson	› Portillo	› Tristan
› Hasselbaink	› Raul	› Van Nistelrooy
› Henry	› Ronaldo	› Viduka
› Inzaghi	› Rooney	› Vieri
› Jardel	› Salas	› Zola

10 POINTS FOR FINDING ALL THE NAMES!

DREAM TEAM

See if ya can work out the top players wot make up this blingin' team!

GK Turkish shot-stopper who likes to wear black make-up under his eyes.

RB Bald-headed Leeds full-back who has a history of getting in trouble with referees.

CB England ace who joined Birmingham from Arsenal last season.

CB Liverpool and Finland defender who is also the club captain at Anfield.

LB Real Madrid pocket-rocket who fancies himself as a free-kick king.

RM England captain who left Manchester United for £25 million at the end of last season.

CM Newcastle's young midfield ace who joined The Magpies from Nottingham Forest.

CM Tough-tackling little AC Milan midfielder who helped them win the European Cup in 2003, and who used to play for Rangers.

LM Republic Of Ireland winger whose surname rhymes with 'tough'.

ST Everton wonderkid who is sometimes called Roonaldo by his fans.

ST Southampton and England striker who scored bags of goals in 2002-03, helping The Saints to the FA Cup final in Cardiff.

1 POINT PER CORRECT ANSWER (MAXIMUM 11)

MATCH

WORLD SUPERSTARS

Harry Kewell ★ Australia

61
Your team lifts the World Cup and you win the Golden Boot. You're almost at the finish now!
Move to square 64

62

63
You're all set to leave Inter and go back to Spain, but the fans get on your back – calling you disloyal!
Go back to square 42

64

65

60

59

58
As you head off to the 2002 World Cup, you decide to get a ridiculous haircut. Doh!
Go back to square 24

57

56

41

42

43

44
You're banging in the goals at Barça, and earn yourself a mega-money move to Inter Milan! Mamma mia!
Move to 56

45

40
Finally, a big club makes a move – and you're off to Barcelona!
Move to square 43

39

38

37

INTER
1908

36

21

22

23

24

25
The freezing weather in Holland is really getting you down!
Go back to square 16

20
While still only 17 years old, you make your Brazil debut and are labelled 'The New Pele'. Wow!
Take an extra turn

19

18
You're banging the goals in and earn yourself a blingin' new contract. Get in!
Move to square 23

17

16

START
Have you got what it takes to be the best? Go for it, footy dudes!

2

3
At the age of 17, you're spotted by scouts from Dutch side PSV and leave Brazil in search of fame!
Move to square 17

PSV

4

5

66
Your move to Madrid finally goes through and you join up with all their other superstars!
Move to the finish

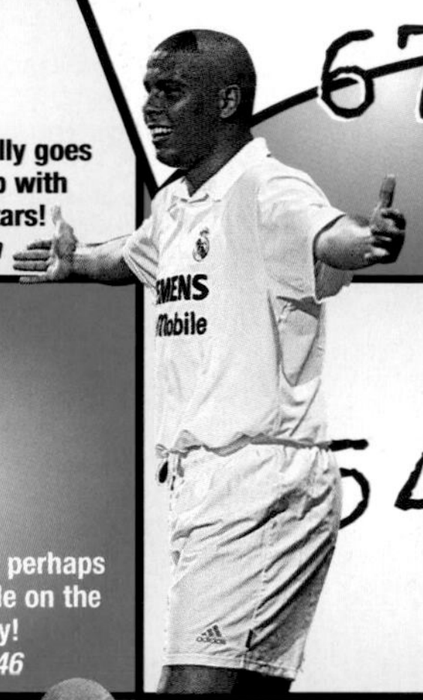

67

68
The Barça fans aren't happy about you playing for their fierce rivals!
Go back to square 54

69

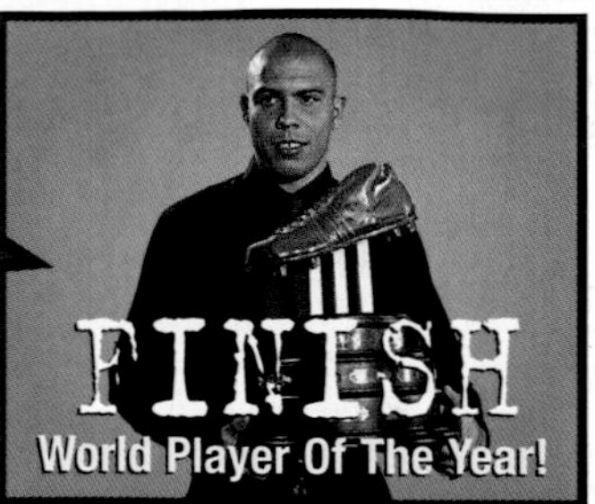

FINISH
World Player Of The Year!

55
You love your lifestyle, but perhaps a bit too much and you pile on the pounds. Sort it, fatty!
Go back to square 46

54

53

52

51
You seem to have shaken off all your injury problems and you're ready to rip it up at the World Cup. 'Ave it!
Move to square 53

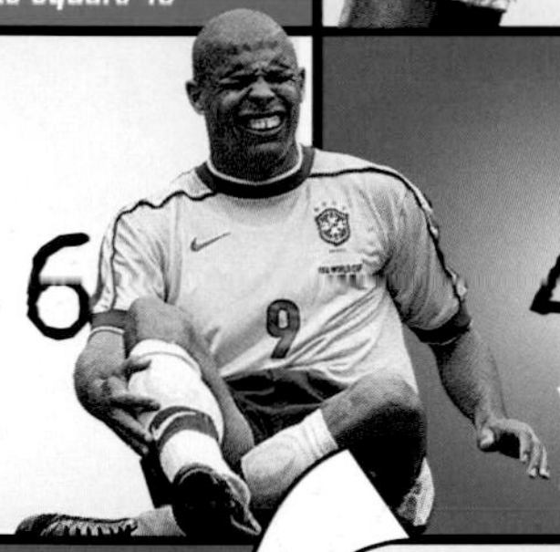

46

47
You pick up your first big injury. Gutted!
Go back to square 35

48

49

50

35

34
Your team-mates get jealous of all the attention you're getting and refuse to pass to you!
Miss a turn

33

32

31

26

27

28

29
Your good form has started to attract the attention of some of Europe's top clubs!
Move to square 33

30

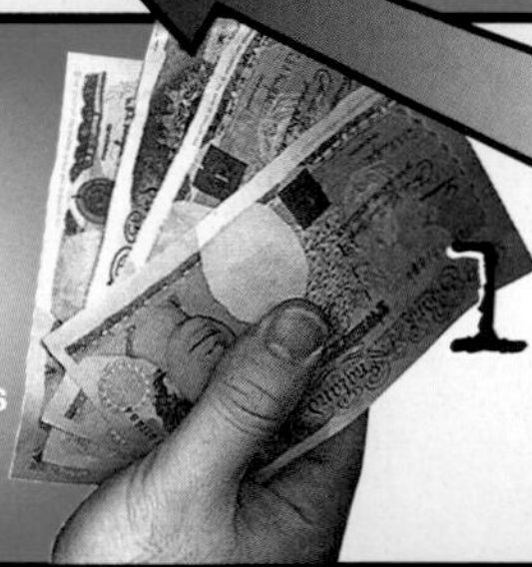

15
They sign you up for loads of wonga – you're really in the money now!
Take an extra turn

14

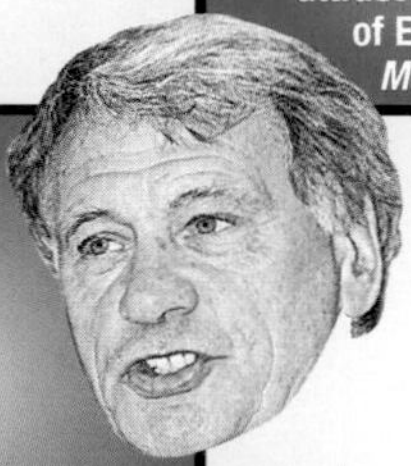

13
You get to work with a great manager like Bobby Robson and your game really improves!
Move to square 26

12

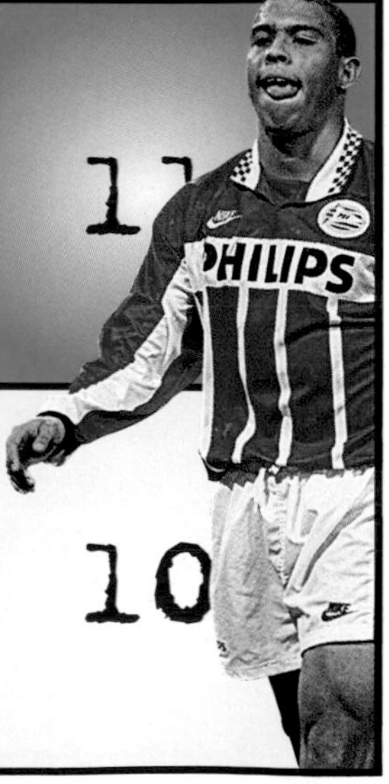

11

6

7

8

9
Learning a new language is tough and it takes time to settle in!
Go back to square 7

10

91

THE BIG MATCH QUIZ
ANSWERS

Okay footy dudes, here's where we separate the genuine fans from the armchair fans! On this page, write down your answers from the five quiz pages earlier in the annual, then add up your points total out of 300 to find out what kind of trophy you've won! Are you a World Cup winner or out the door on a free transfer? Total up your score now to find out!

261-300
YOU'VE WON THE WORLD CUP!

A star in the making! Anything over the 261 mark rates you as a very special footy brain. You must go to every game and your head's pretty much a portable footy encyclopedia. Watch out though, all your mates are gonna be after you for the latest gossip and info!

221-260
YOU'VE WON THE CHAMPIONS LEAGUE!

A top performance! Okay, so you haven't claimed footy's top prize, but you've shown you've got well above the normal amount of talent. Just a bit of hard work and more reading of MATCH, and you should be at the pinnacle of being a footy fan!

176-220
YOU'VE WON THE FA CUP!

You deserve credit! A solid showing that marks you out as well worthy of a mention, but you may have had a little bit of luck on the way. Don't give up though, you're not at your peak yet and anyone that can win the FA Cup is still pretty special!

131-175
YOU'VE WON THE LEAGUE CUP!

Good, but not brilliant! Okay, so it's still silverware, but you've really got to be aiming higher than this. You need a bit of polishing up on your footy facts to get the really big, flash trophies. Keep at it though – and you never know!

86-130
YOU'VE WON THE SECOND DIVISION!

Oh dear! You have to admit this isn't anything special! The only positive to take is you're still young and you can work hard at your game, but that's about it! This is going to be a real test of your character, because you need to read MATCH a lot more!

41-85
YOU'VE WON THE LDV VANS TROPHY!

Oh well, you had a nice day out! Let's face it, no-one really cares about the LDV Vans Trophy, do they? It's the bargain basement consolation prize for you, we're afraid. Keep at it, but we're not holding out much hope for next year. You must try harder!

under 40
YOU'VE WON A FREE TRANSFER!

You're out of here! Too bad buddy. You had your big chance – but too many easy errors spelled the end for you. We can't work out why you even attempted this quiz in the first place. Under 40 is awful – the door's that way pal, and don't come back!

Big Match Quiz One — page 26

FIRST XI (1 point each)

1	
2	
3	
4	
5	
6	
7	
8	
9	
10	
11	

1. 1899; 2. True; 3. Andriy Shevchenko; 4. Six; 5. Lazio; 6. Inter Milan; 7. Patrick Vieira; 8. Paolo Maldini 9. Ruud Gullit; 10. Silvio Berlusconi; 11. False.

FREAK OR UNIQUE! (2 points)

| 1 | |

False.

KIT KINGS (2 points)

| 1 | |

Aston Villa.

GROUND FORCE (2 points)

| 1 | |

Madrid.

SPELL CHECK STARS (2 points each)

1	
2	
3	

1. Juninho; 2. Ronaldinho; 3. Gilberto Silva.

EYE EYE! (2 points each)

1	
2	
3	
4	
5	

1. Michael Owen; 2. Jimmy Floyd Hasselbaink; 3. Thierry Henry; 4. Robbie Keane; 5. Ole Gunnar Solskjaer.

THE NICKNAME GAME (1 point each)

1	
2	
3	
4	
5	

1D; 2C; 3E; 4A; 5B.

CAP IN HAND (5 points)

| 1 | |

b) 80.

Big Match Quiz Two — page 44

SECOND XI (1 point each)

1	
2	
3	
4	
5	
6	
7	
8	
9	
10	
11	

1. Pele; 2. 1958; 3. Germany; 4. True; 5. Five; 6. 1950; 7. Italy; 8. False (it was Ronaldo's girlfriend); 9. Atletico Minerio; 10. Blue; 11. Rivaldo.

SPELL CHECK STARS (2 points each)

1	
2	
3	

1. Brad Friedel; 2. Paul Konchesky; 3. Darius Vassel.

TRANSFER TRACKER (3 points)

| 1 | |

deep Stam.

BALL GAMES (10 points for correct answer)

1	
2	
3	
4	
5	
6	
ANSWER=	

1. Juventus; 2. Saints; 3. Shola; 4. Arsenal; 5. Leeds; 6. Sinclair. (Answer= Vieri).

LEGS ELEVEN (2 points each)

| 1 | |
| 2 | |

1. Jermaine Jenas; 2. Joe Cole.

ALPHABET QUIZ (2 points each)

1	
2	
3	

1. Tugay; 2. Terriers; 3. Taylor.

ANAGRAMS (2 points each)

1	
2	
3	
4	
5	

1. Emile Heskey; 2. Gareth Southgate; 3. Chris Marsden; 4. Frank Lampard; 5. Gary Neville.

SOL CAMPBELL QUIZ (2 points each)

1.
2.
3.
4.
5.

1. 1974; 2. True; 3. Arsenal; 4. 2001; 5. Sweden.

Big Match Quiz Three — page 54

THIRD XI (1 point each)

1.
2.
3.
4.
5.
6.
7.
8.
9.
10.
11.

1. Sir Alf Ramsey; 2. True; 3. Ruud Gullit; 4. Jamie; 5. True; 6. 1996; 7. Trevor Brooking; 8. Preston North End; 9. Tord Grip; 10. True; 11. One.

THOSE WERE THE DAYS (3 points)

1.

Michael Owen.

JUAN VERON QUIZ (2 points each)

1.
2.
3.
4.
5.

1. £28.1 million; 2. Everton; 3. The Little Witch; 4. True; 5. 28.

WHO IS MR POTATO? (4 points)

1.

Mark Viduka.

PLAYER MATCH-UP (2 points each)

1.
2.
3.
4.
5.
6.

1C; 2A; 3E; 4F; 5B; 6D.

KIT KINGS (2 points)

1.

Liverpool.

WHO AM I? (5 points)

1.

Frank Lampard.

TABLE TOPPERS (2 points)

1.

1993.

DREAM TEAM (1 point each)

GK	
RB	
CB	
CB	
LB	
RM	
CM	
CM	
LM	
ST	
ST	

GK Oliver Kahn; RB Cafu; CB Rio Ferdinand; CB Alessandro Nesta; LB John Arne Riise; RM Luis Figo; CM Simon Davies; CM Michael Ballack; LM Pavel Nedved; ST Alan Shearer; ST Christian Vieri.

Big Match Quiz Four — page 66

FOURTH XI (1 point each)

1.
2.
3.
4.
5.
6.
7.
8.
9.
10.
11.

1. The Bernabeu; 2. £48 million; 3. No.5 shirt; 4. C; 5. A; 6. Eight; 7. Steve McManaman; 8. Spain; 9. Barcelona; 10. False; 11. Gerrard.

FREAK OR UNIQUE! (3 points)

1.

False.

KIT KINGS (4 points)

1.

Fulham.

SPOT THE DIFFERENCE! (2 points each)

1.
2.
3.
4.
5.

1. Umbro logo on Owen's top; 2. No.7 on Slovakian's shorts; 3. Blue stripe missing on Owen's sock; 4. Mitre logo on ball; 5. Slovakian player wearing No.8 shirt.

PLAYER MATCH-UP (2 points each)

1.
2.
3.
4.
5.

1E; 2D; 3B; 4A; 5C.

SAY WHAT? (2 points)

1.

David Beckham.

ONE OF A KIND (3 points)

1.

Carlos.

CAP IN HAND (5 points)

1.

(B) 45.

NAFF NOSES! (2 points each)

1.
2.
3.
4.
5.
6.

1. Kieron Dyer; 2. Roy Keane; 3. Patrick Vieira; 4. Sami Hyypia; 5. Gianfranco Zola; 6. James Beattie.

Big Match Quiz Five — page 88

FIFTH XI (1 point each)

1.
2.
3.
4.
5.
6.
7.
8.
9.
10.
11.

1. Ron Atkinson; 2. Nottingham Forest; 3. South Africa; 4. C; 10. 5. Eight; 6. PSV Eindhoven; 7. True; 8. Reading; 9. True; 10. Jaap Stam; 11. Mark Hughes.

GROUND FORCE (1 point)

1.

Manchester City (Maine Road).

WHO AM I? (1 point)

1.

Ray Parlour.

ALPHABET QUIZ (2 points each)

1.
2.
3.
4.
5.

1. Dublin; 2. Deportivo; 3. Derby; 4. Dudek; 5. Denmark.

GOALMOUTH SCRAMBLE (1 point each)

Any 15 from: able, amp, ample, ball, bell, cab, call, cap, label, lace, lamb, lamp, lap, leap, map, maple, meal, pace.

CAP IN HAND (1 point)

1.

(A) 63.

DREAM TEAM (1 point each)

GK	
RB	
CB	
CB	
LB	
RM	
CM	
CM	
LM	
ST	
ST	

GK Rushi Recber; RB Danny Mills; CB Matthew Upson; CB Sami Hyypia; LB Roberto Carlos; RM David Beckham; CM Jermaine Jenas; CM Gennaro Gattuso; LM Damien Duff; ST Wayne Rooney; ST James Beattie.

WORD FIT – BIG MATCH QUIZ 1

Out of 20 points I scored...

MEGA WORDSPOT – BIG MATCH QUIZ 5

10 points for all! I scored...

FOOTY

JOKES!

Impress your pals with these gags...

OUT OF THIS WORLD!

> Why will you never see any football stadiums in outer space?

> *Because there's no atmosphere up there!*

SAME OLD STADIUM!

> Which part of a footy stadium is never the same from one day to the next?

> *The changing rooms!*

BLAME MUM AND DAD!

> Three footy fans are moaning about their fave team, who always lose. "I blame the gaffer," says the first. "If he'd signed better players, we'd be okay." The second pipes up: "I blame the players. If they made more effort we wouldn't be in this mess." "Nah, I blame my parents," the third fan says. "If I'd been born in another town, I'd support a decent footy team!"

MESSY EATERS!

> Why don't footballers get invited out to dinner?

> *Because they dribble everywhere they go!*

TACTICS PUT-DOWN!

> When the gaffer mentioned tactics, you thought he was talking about a packet of mints!

REFFY NO MATES!

> Three strangers arrive at the annual football club dance. The bouncer stops them at the door and asks to see their tickets. "But we haven't got tickets," says one of the strangers. "We're friends with the referee!" The bouncer looks at them closely and says: "You think I believe that? Who's ever heard of a referee with friends?"

11 REASONS WHY....

...footy is the wickedest sport in the world – ever!

1 You don't need a net, a bat, a club or a racket to play football – you don't even need a pitch! Just grab a ball, a couple of jumpers for goalposts and you're away! Just make sure you use your own jumper and not your dad's cardigan!

2 It doesn't matter if it's raining, snowing, windy or hailing – you can play footy whatever the weather. Not like those wimpy cricketers, who stop their rubbish game at the first sign of rain!

3 Football is a universal language! You can go to almost any country in the world and – even if you can't speak the lingo – make friends straight away by having a kickabout with the locals!

4 Playing plenty of footy keeps you fit and healthy – except for when your mum goes mad because all your best clothes are caked in mud. Urrggh!

5 You can get wicked footy games for your computer – and dribble past your mate's players with your 'keeper before sticking the ball in the net. 'Ave it!

6 There are loads of famous football stadiums like the Bernabeu, the San Siro, Anfield, Old Trafford and the Millennium Stadium. And when the new Wembley opens in a couple of years, that should be a well cool ground too!

7 The World Cup takes place every four years – so you can take over the telly in your house for a month! That really annoys your sister and your mum, coz they can't watch stuff like EastEnders and Coronation Street. Quality, eh?

8 The Premiership only runs from August to May, but there are still loads of wicked footy tournaments in the summer months – like the Confederations Cup and the European Championships!

9 Transfer gossip rules! Half of it may be rubbish, but tennis, cricket or rugby players don't get linked with Real Madrid and Inter Milan, do they?

10 It's the most entertaining game in the world, with fab tricksters like Jay-Jay Okocha, crazy clowns like Fabien Barthez and style icons like Dave Becks!

11 Without footy there'd be no MATCH – just imagine that! It would mean no blingin' interviews with all the best players, no Planet Footy, no fun quizzes and no MATCHMAN! What a nightmare!

Congratulations – you've reached the end of the MATCH annual!
We hope you've enjoyed the read, and that your brain is ready to burst with footy knowledge! After learning how the world's best strikers made it to the top, testing yourself in the quizzes and laughing at Planet Footy, you should know loads about footy! Last season was wicked, but the 2003-04 campaign will be even better! With the climax to the Premiership title race and the Euro 2004 championships to come, it's gonna be a year to remember. And you can keep up-to-date with all the stars, interviews and news in MATCH every Tuesday! You can write to us at MATCH, Bushfield House, Orton Centre, Peterborough, PE2 5UW. See ya footy dudes!